La Quinta
Legend In The Making

Victoria J. Bailey

DESERT SPRINGS PUBLISHING

2007

DESERT SPRINGS PUBLISHING

Victoria J. Bailey, Publisher

Joan Fitzgerald, Associate Publisher

Gayl Biondi, Editorial Director

Becky Kurtz, Editorial Consultant

Karen Oppenheim, Contributing Writer

CONTRIBUTING PHOTOGRAPHS

City of La Quinta, La Quinta Historical Society,
La Quinta Resort & Club, PGA WEST,
La Quinta Arts Foundation, La Quinta County Club

CONTRIBUTING PHOTOGRAPHY

Steven Weiner, Marc Glassman, Mark Stephenson, John Kirkpatrick, Evan Schiller,
Tom Kennedy, John Weidehamer, Brian Maurer and Terry L. Deeinger

DESIGN AND PRODUCTION

Eaton & Kirk Advertising
John Kirkpatrick, Creative Director; Ramsey Lucas, Graphic Designer

COVER DESIGN

John Kirkpatrick, Eaton & Kirk Advertising,
large central photo courtesy Terry L. Deeinger

Desert Springs Publishing

78-365 Highway 111, Suite 340, La Quinta, CA 92253

760-219-7008

victoria@desertspringspublishing.com

www.desertspringspublishing.com

Eaton & Kirk Advertising

47-159 Youngs Lane, Indio, CA 92201

760-775-3626

info@eatonkirk.com • www.eatonkirk.com

ISBN # 0-9727572-4-4
Library of Congress Control Number: 2007901248
© Copyright 2007 by Desert Springs Publishing

Published 2007, Printed in China by Toppan Printing Company

Table of Contents

ELMO OLIVER

PHOTOGRAPHER MARK STEPHENSON

PHOTOGRAPHER STEVEN WEINER

Acknowledgement

Twenty-five years is not long in the history of a City, but La Quinta's heritage has a rich legacy which goes back to the turn of the 19th Century when land grants of 160 acre parcels were given out to homesteaders who would receive title to this land after five years.

From this humble beginning, the City of La Quinta, — this "Gem of the Desert" — has appeared and those of us who are fortunate enough to live here can reap the benefit of the people before us who had what I call "infinite vision" to build this wonderful community. This book is a memorial to those marvelous people that shaped our future.

I would like to thank the hard working staff of the City of La Quinta, the City Council Members and the staff of the following organizations that provided me with history, photos, and support. They are the La Quinta Historical Society Museum, La Quinta Arts Foundation, La Quinta Resort and Club, PGA WEST and La Quinta Country Club.

"La Quinta - Legend In The Making" is my contribution to the future history of this special place. This book could not have happened without the efforts of my team; Gay Biondi, Karen Oppenheim and the design team at Eaton & Kirk.

I would also like to thank those businesses that participated with their stories about the past, present and future. These are businesses that will help the city prosper with their growth and community involvement.

I have lived in La Quinta since 2002 and I cherish the many friends that I have made in the community and it is with heartfelt gratitude that I dedicate this book to all of them who gave so generously of their time. As a storyteller, this has been one of my favorite tales.

— *Victoria J. Bailey, Publisher*

SilverRock Resort, Arnold Palmer Classic Course, Hole #18

PHOTOGRAPHER EVAN SCHILLER

Forward

"I have had the opportunity to live in La Quinta for many years and have always enjoyed playing golf here. I send my congratulations on the occasion of this wonderful 25th anniversary celebration. What a great job City officials and the citizens of La Quinta have done in promoting the best interests of the desert resort area. I have been privileged to build the SilverRock Resort golf course for the City and certainly think that it will be known as one of La Quinta's proudest assets for years to come."

— Arnold Palmer

The occasion of the City's 25th Anniversary is a perfect time to celebrate La Quinta's tremendous accomplishments. The La Quinta story has actually been thousands of years in the making. Once under the waters of ancient Lake Cahuilla, the place we call La Quinta has always been a place of great discovery.

La Quinta. The name itself is the stuff of legends. In Spanish, "quint" translates as "villa or country house; draft or military conscription; or sequence of five." So, it is little wonder there are several interpretations of how the city of La Quinta got its name.

One legend says early Western explorers who rode by horseback would push along for four days with little rest. On the fifth night (called "la quint") they would relax and set up camp, enjoying food and drink, giving their horses respite. The anticipation of the good times waiting at the regular fifth stop on the journey made it "a special place."

The more enduring legend has it that Walter Morgan, the wealthy San Francisco aristocrat who came to the desert in 1921 for health reasons, purchased 1,400 acres to create a secluded retreat where guests could "take the sun" and be pampered in seclusion. Morgan was told by a local rancher that in Old Mexico, a man's country home (or quint) was typically named after his wife to favor her.

Thus, "La Quinta Rosa" would be how the husband of a woman named Rosa would refer to their family getaway spot. Mr. Morgan is said to have loved the visual imagery of a beautiful main house (or hacienda) surrounded by guest houses (or casitas) and gardens. To give all guests the feeling that this hotel was their special place, he christened his venture the La Quinta Hotel.

In 1990, then-President of the La Quinta Historical Society Fred Rice took the sentiment one step further when he said, "I call it Shangri-La Quinta." No matter how the place got its name, everyone seems to agree that La Quinta has always been and will always be a special place both in the world and in the heart.

— *Gayl Biondi, Editorial Director*

CHAPTER ONE

An early painting of the La Quinta cove bungalows, circa 1930.

Discovery of an Earthbound Eden

ELMO OLIVER

 It couldn't have been easy - pioneering a desert landscape that was often unforgiving and prone to flash floods, epic windstorms, and searing heat. Yet they came, they stayed, and they flourished. And what they found, over time, was that this place - La Quinta - was ripe with opportunity and promise.

The first applications for land grants in La Quinta were recorded at the turn of the century. Homesteaders could enter claims for up to 160 acres and receive title after five years of residence and cultivation. Records show that 73 land grants were patented. With the arrival of the early homesteaders came the beginning of both the hospitality and agriculture industries that continue to fuel our local economy.

Forces of Nature

"We believe La Quinta was the cradle of civilization where human life began on Earth." That was the simple but profound legend put forth by Katherine Siva Saubel, a historian for the Cahuilla Indians, the first people known to inhabit what we call the Coachella Valley. Remnants of Cahuilla culture may still be found in pottery shards, fish traps, and rock paintings near the Santa Rosa Mountains in La Quinta's backyard.

The stage was set by forces of nature around the San Andreas Fault. The Santa Rosa Mountains were formed by two plates in the Earth's crust pushing against each other. An ancient sea once covered the entire Coachella Valley. Oyster and mollusk shells can still be found in rocks thrust upward by seismic activity near Thousand Palms and Indio Hills. Continued upheaval and silt deposits from the Colorado River eventually caused the sea to subside.

When the mighty Colorado changed its course during a heavy flood season, it created a freshwater lake - ancient Lake Cahuilla - that spanned 2,000 square miles and covered the eastern valley floor to a depth of 40 feet above sea level. Native Americans used mountain trails as their transportation system to traverse the high and low country that made up their domain. From Sugar Loaf in the mountains near Idyllwild, Bear Creek Trail led them down the mountain to what is now La Quinta.

The line of demarcation between the Pass Cahuilla tribe and the Desert Cahuilla tribe was thought to be where La Quinta sits today. In winter, the clan lived in the shelter of the cove, where warm, easterly winds provided a moderate climate. The men fished and hunted along the lakeshore. The women gathered vegetation and seed pods. In summer, they moved up into the canyons to take advantage of cool drafts created by heat rising from the desert floor.

Bear Creek Trail Today

Tom Kennedy's Olla

Artifacts such as ollas, or ancient kettles made of clay, are still found around the base of the Santa Rosa Mountains. This one measures two feet high and 18 inches in diameter and was reconstructed by longtime La Quinta resident Tom Kennedy, when he was nine years old, from pieces he discovered while hiking along Washington Street near Avenue 50. The young Kennedy painstakingly reconstructed the Indian olla like a puzzle with over 250 pieces. Kennedy was often rewarded for pursuing his amateur archeology pastime. "I was out one day after a high wind," he says, "and an amulet was lying right on top of the ground. It had been there for hundreds of years just waiting for the sand to shift and uncover it."

Cahuilla historians report that the last large lake recalled by their ancestors was approximately 500 years ago. Records of Spanish explorers confirm that the lake was gone by 1540. When survey geologist William Blake explored the area in 1853, he was quoted as saying, "I saw a discoloration of the rocks extending for a long distance in a horizontal line on the side of the mountains. These evidences of a former submergence were so vivid and conclusive that it became evident to everyone that we were traveling in the dry bed of a former deep and extended sheet of water, probably an ancient lake or extensive bay."

Lake Cahuilla's Shoreline Watermark

The watermark can still be seen today along the mountains south of La Quinta. What geologists call calcareous incrustations are mixtures of calcium carbonate and magnesium hydroxide deposited in areas of increased pH. We commonly refer to the luminous coating as coral reef and the white crust as tufa. To preserve what's left of the area's rich archeological remains, the Bureau of Reclamation and the Coachella Valley Recreation and Parks District have designated 600 acres for the Valley's first archeological park, with interpretive trails, picnic areas and a trailhead. The site is near the southwest corner of Madison Street and Avenue 58.

Martinez Slide

Carl Bock, a Bechtel engineer on assignment with the Coachella Valley Water District, was the first to document the Martinez Mountain rockslide as one of the largest in the United States. It covers 5.2 miles, and debris is 180 feet deep in places. The mass of material released in the slide covers nearly 2000 acres, or 3 square miles. Boulders 55 feet long and 20 feet high were noted. The total volume of the slide is close to 500 million cubic feet.

Cal Tech scientists have confirmed evidence of at least four earthquakes in the Coachella Valley capable of creating such a massive slide - around the years 800, 1250, 1500 and 1680. Evidence of wave action on parts of the slide suggests it happened before the 1680 event, by which time ancient Lake Cahuilla was already gone.

The Martinez Slide is now confirmed to be the second largest rockslide in North America and the fifth largest in the world. It can be seen south of Avenue 60 on the east-facing slope of the Santa Rosa Mountains, behind Trilogy Country Club.

Cahuilla Found Bounty in the Desert

The Cahuilla led a modest existence in the arid desert, yet they saw beauty and value in all things, giving human characteristics to the forces of nature around them. They called their Garden of Eden, "The Palm of God's Hand." Historians point out that the Cahuilla were not a nomadic people. Villages tended to be permanent, and occupancy transferred to succeeding generations of the clan lineage.

The Cahuilla were one of the few Native American tribes to dig wells. The original Indian well that gave the city of Indian Wells its name was located less than 300 yards from the current intersection of Highway 111 and Washington Street in La Quinta, near the Cliffhouse restaurant.

The first contact the native Cahuillas had with outsiders was 16th Century Spanish explorers, or conquistadors, searching for riches. One source indicates the name "La Quinta" was first associated with this location in 1774 by Captain Juan Bautista D'Anza during his quest to find an overland route from Sonora, Mexico to the San Gabriel Mission and Monterey.

There were approximately 20 villages in the Desert Cahuilla territory. The two that are associated with La Quinta were Kavinish, near present-day Washington Street and Highway 111, and Kotevewit, somewhere between the present location of La Quinta Resort and The Tradition. The Cahuilla respected nature as a source of their sustenance. Even though the land was arid, they found what they needed in the plant life around them.

FAN PALM

Leaves were used to thatch roofs of dwellings. Fibers were used to make baskets and sandals. Leaf stems were carved into shovels and spoons. Tips were eaten as food. Palm fruit was eaten fresh, sun-dried and stored, ground into flour or used to make tea.

PHOTO COURTESY OF PALM SPRINGS HISTORICAL SOCIETY

OCOTILLO

Roots were ground into powder and mixed with warm water to make a soothing bath to relieve fatigue, steeped as tea said to reduce the moist cough of elders, and powdered to apply to joints to reduce swelling. Branches were used as firewood, or stuck upright into the ground close to each other and watered every few days to create a living fence to keep rabbits out of gardens. Blossoms were mixed with water for a tasty drink, or wilted to collect the seeds to grind into flour and mix with water to form small cakes.

MESQUITE

Fruit pods were crushed and mixed with water to be eaten as mush, or made into cakes to be dried. Flowers were roasted and pressed into balls to eat, or boiled for tea. Leaves were used to make medicinal tea. Leaves and twigs were ground into a poultice to be used on cuts or scratches. Sap was used as an adhesive. Trunks were hollowed out and used as mortar for grinding. Branches were used to make bows.

Bradshaw Trail

By 1862, the Civil War was raging, and gold was needed to finance guns and ammo for both the North and the South. As luck would have it, a frontiersman on a trapping expedition stumbled upon a gold deposit along the Colorado River in Arizona. Once word got out about the strike, a safe, direct route from the California coast to the Colorado River was in great demand.

elder. The Chief agreed to show Bradshaw the Indian trail to the Colorado River to prevent gold prospectors from lingering in the area long enough to steal scarce food and water from his people.

Bradshaw was happy to take credit for the trail he boasted would save 200 miles and 10 days of travel. Over half of the route ran through the Coachella Valley, and past the Point Happy homestead. The Bradshaw Stage Line got off to a rocky start. On its first trip carrying passengers back from the New Mexico Territory with $5,000 in gold, the stage was

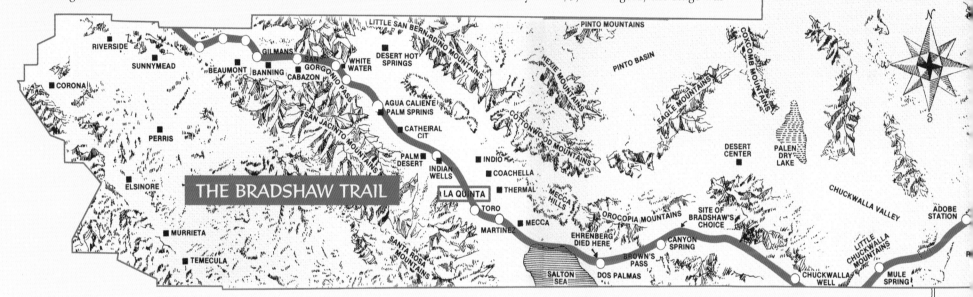

William Bradshaw, an educated and experienced guide, soldier and miner, was chosen to blaze the new trail. In May of the same year, Bradshaw and party set out east from San Bernardino. When they reached the Cahuilla settlement of Toro Village, located southeast of present-day La Quinta, Bradshaw encountered Chief Cabazon, the tribal

robbed in the Banning Pass and everyone was killed. The stage did not run again for five years, until the route was officially authorized by the U.S. Congress as a mail route.

The Bradshaw Stage Line passed through La Quinta until 1877. With the coming of the railroad, travel by stagecoach was going out of favor. The segment of the stage line that passed through La Quinta was replaced by a graded gravel road in 1915. Much of the old Bradshaw trail that ran through Southern California became the foundation for modern Interstate 10.

Point Happy Ranch

We can only assume that Norman "Happy" Lundbeck ignored those who called him eccentric when he homesteaded land for a small trading post sometime before 1900. The location he picked was already a landmark on the 1884 Rand McNally map, indicated by a large alluvial fan bordered by a mesquite forest. It was a crossroads for Indians, prospectors, traders and assorted privateers riding the discovery trail.

Stagecoaches and freight wagons stopped at the nearby watering hole, and took refuge in the shadow of the Santa Rosa mountain spur when fierce sandstorms or dangerous flash floods came roaring down the valley from the west. Happy Lundbeck stabled horses and offered provisions to weary travelers. The busy crossing at the mountain spur near the intersection of present-day Washington Street and Highway 111 soon became known as Point Happy.

Point Happy was purchased in 1922 by Chauncey Clarke, a wealthy oil man, geologist and philanthropist, and his wife, Marie. Clarke had a passion for two things bred in the deserts of the Old World - Arabian horses and dates. He believed the conditions at Point Happy were ideal to farm dates and raise horses that were "sure-footed and strong." Eleven of the original Davenport bloodline of Arabians were collected at Point Happy Ranch. One of them, Jadaan, became famous as the on-screen steed of silent-screen heartthrob Rudolph Valentino.

Clarke named the 135-acre ranch Point Happy Date Gardens and cultivated the first Deglet Noor (translated as "date of light") dates in California. The *Los Angeles Times* reported, "Mr. Clarke's ideas of selecting the desert of Southern California as the ideal place is the result of many years of experience and observation. With Mrs. Clarke, he has traveled all over the world, and his outstanding reason for the selection of this location is that it is nearest to Arabia in climatic respects, and nearest also to the greatest outdoor playground of the world, Southern California."

BY FRED RICE

THE POINT HAPPY RANCH

Rudolph Valentino
Riding a white Arabian in the desert.

First School

The Point Happy School District was formed in 1892 to serve students from "halfway to Palm Springs and two miles east of Washington Street." Records from 1916 show that one teacher was paid $440 to teach seven pupils for a 160-day school year. In 1924, Edith Wild White took over as teacher. She kept a library of legal and medical reference texts, and was often consulted by farmers and townspeople.

The Clarkes' money and influence attracted an A-list of celebrities and political leaders to the ranch, including Greta Garbo, William Powell, Clark Gable, and even President Taft, all of whom were known to frequent the La Quinta Hotel nearby. Louise Neeley grew up on the ranch, while her father served as a ranch foreman and her mother kept the Clarkes' house.

Says Neeley, "The Clarkes' guests got to know us kids pretty well. We splashed around the guesthouse pool, played house under the grapefruit trees in the garden and had the run of the place."

In addition to the date groves, the Clarkes maintained citrus trees, row crops and sugar cane. Irrigation was handled by artesian wells, using electric and diesel pumps. Mrs. Clarke's full time gardener, Mr. Akahoshi, planted a large vegetable garden and maintained an extensive rose garden for the pleasure of the Clarkes and their guests.

When his health began to fail, Chauncey Clarke sold his beloved Arabian horses to the Kellogg Ranch in Pomona, where they became the breeding stock of the purebred Arabian in California. He died in 1926. Marie Clarke continued to live on the ranch, and became known as "Madame Happy."

Marie Clarke was a founder of the Hollywood Bowl, and was instrumental in underwriting the Indio Women's Club. At her death in 1948, Mrs. Clarke left the ranch to Claremont College, which, in turn, sold off parts of the property.

The Point Happy Date Gardens was purchased in the mid-1950s by William DuPont, Jr., then CEO of the DuPont Chemical Corporation. DuPont loved the dry desert climate and the serene beauty of the La Quinta cove. He is also rumored to have enjoyed the exquisite cuisine and club-like atmosphere of the La Quinta Hotel, where many of his fellow captains of industry held court along with Hollywood celebrities.

To best enjoy his desert digs, DuPont built a house on top of the mountain saddle overlooking the ranch. The added elevation gave him an unobstructed view in each direction. In 1965, DuPont added a Mediterranean-style house with its own swimming pool and tennis court for 1930s tennis champion, Alice Marble, near his palm grove. The house was finished on December 26th; DuPont died on December 29th.

Point Happy Ranch

Picking Dates

A young Louise Neeley picks fruit from a date palm at Point Happy Ranch.

Poolside

Mrs. Clarke and guests gather poolside on the lawn during a cloudy day in November, 1941. Navajo rugs are spread around the pool.

Early Ranchos

Southern Pacific Railroad had completed its transcontinental route in 1876, bringing even more curious spectators and speculators to the area. Sporadic homesteading started to take hold as folks got caught up in the pioneer spirit. Two of the early adopters were brothers-in-law John Marshall and Albert Green.

HACIENDA DEL GATO

Together, they homesteaded 320 acres, raising citrus and date palms along present-day Avenue 52. The only known prehistoric cemetery

Original ranch gates were incorporated into Hole #3

in the Valley was unearthed at Marshall Ranch. Upon John Marshall's arrival, what we know as Washington Street was called Marshall Road, and the area where The Tradition is today was called Marshall's Cove.

Early farmers like Marshall had to rely on pumps and hand-dug wells to supply their crops with water. John Marshall met an untimely death on the ranch in 1938 when an old pit caved in on him.

The Marshall Ranch was sold to William Rosencrans, a well-to-do tycoon from Los Angeles. Supposedly, a family cat prevented a rattlesnake from striking Mrs. Rosencrans, so the couple renamed the property Hacienda del Gato (house of the cat). The ranch was eventually sold again to Fritz Burns, a land developer and builder responsible for numerous post-World War II housing tracts in Los Angeles and the San Fernando Valley.

The cat took on yet another of its nine lives when Hacienda del Gato transferred hands again in 1954 to James Holmes. He banished the dying date palms in favor of an ambitious estate planted with Washingtonia filifera and robusta palms, bamboo, persimmons, eucalyptus, cottonwoods, pomegranates, jacarandas, Eureka lemons, Seville oranges, pink grapefruits, ruby grapefruits, temple oranges, Dancy tangerines, Valencia oranges, Ponderosa

lemons, Algerian tangerines and cactus. The property remained a working citrus ranch until the death of longtime caretaker, Al Lopez, in 1991.

A host of celebrities and political figures, including John F. Kennedy, are rumored to have visited the ranch. In 1996, the ranch was developed into what has become Tradition Golf Club, under the watchful eyes of partners Arnold Palmer and David Chapman. Arnold Palmer was looking for a western U.S. location to create a championship golf experience in a socially intimate setting. The Hacienda del Gato site, with its awe-inspiring natural setting, caused Palmer to say, "This land is something really wonderful. It bends and curves beautifully, set against the mountains, giving the golf course lots of drama."

Palmer, along with David Chapman and Ed Seay, conceived The Tradition as a place for splendid isolation. Natural desert landscaping is generously sprinkled with wildflowers to attract desert wild life. Low density residential development and minimal encroachment have preserved the location's other-worldliness.

The original hacienda, with its wood beam ceilings, lighting fixtures from Spain, and stately trees in the courtyard, remains revered. The original front gates of the former ranch have been preserved at Hole 3 on the golf course.

RANCHO XOCHIMILCO

The stake originally allotted to John Marshall's brother-in-law, Albert Green, in 1902, laid mostly untouched until 1961 when it was purchased by Howard Ahmanson, founder and president of Home Savings and Loan Association, and his wife, Carolyn Leonetti. The gentleman rancher built a house, guest house, manager's house, and outbuildings. The house featured beamed ceilings, hand-carved doors, mosaic tiles designed by a California artist, and a massive, native stone fireplace.

Ahmanson retained a Mexican sculptor to carve replicas of Toltec statues he admired. Noted golf course architect Robert Trent Jones was hired to design a private nine-hole golf course with a waterfall. Ahmanson also raised Hereford cattle and horses, but had to lease additional land to grow enough alfalfa to feed them.

Landmark Land Company bought the property in 1984 and used Ahmanson's ranch house as corporate offices until they sold the land in 1993 to KSL Resorts. The City of La Quinta purchased the property in 2002 with redevelopment funds to create SilverRock Resort as a master-planned golf resort, with golf course architecture by Arnold Palmer.

The SilverRock Retreat and Clubhouse

Built in 1961 as the Howard Ahmanson Family Ranch house
Mr. Ahmanson was the founder of Home Savings & Loan

Purchased by the City's Redevelopment Agency in 2002
and remodeled in 2004 as a vital component of the
SilverRock Resort Project

Mayor Don Adolph
Mayor Pro Tem Stanley Sniff
Council Member Terry Henderson
Council Member Lee Osborne
Council Member Ron Perkins
City Manager Thomas P. Genovese
Project Manager Mark Weiss

**City of La Quinta
Dedication Plaque**

Ahmanson House
The residence is now the SilverRock Resort Clubhouse.

Toltec Statues
These statues are a signature element of the grounds.

Comrades In Farms

On the home front, a number of pioneers developed deep roots both in the soil and the social fabric of La Quinta. Ranch life was hard, but local families made their marks on the tight-knit community by pitching in to help each other. Some still have ties to La Quinta today.

BURKETT RANCH

Manning Burkett homesteaded an area one mile from the current intersection of Highway 111 and Washington Street. A finish carpenter by trade, he helped build the La Quinta Hotel but quit the job (which included room and board) because they served cornflakes three times a day. He later worked for Mr. Clarke on the Point Happy Ranch, building stables for the Arabian horses. Five generations of Burketts lived on their ranch until it was torn down in 1996. A plaque honoring the Burkett Family's accomplishments is on display at the Palm Desert National Bank branch on Washington Street and Avenue 47.

PEDERSON RANCH

Ray Pederson farmed what is now the residential development of Lake La Quinta. Over the years, the land was used to raise everything from tomatoes, beans, squash, peas and dates to gladiolas. The produce and flowers were harvested and sent to market in Los Angeles.

Another part of his land too dense with clay for farming became a private landing strip for the rich and famous who flew to the La Quinta Hotel. The airport had four 2200 foot runways.

Gladiola Harvesting

La Quinta Private Airport

Planes owned by members of the Aviation Country Club of California.

Burketts

Aunt Lottie and Manning Burkett with grandsons Bill and Jack on the ranch that is now Lake La Quinta residential development.

VAIDEN RANCH

Fred Ickes came to the Valley in the 1920s and planted dates and citrus where The Enclave is today. Ickes' brother-in-law, Mead Vaiden, had an engineering degree from Cornell, but decided to come to La Quinta to grow dates on a ranch near Eisenhower and Tampico. Clinton Hunt was a college buddy of Vaiden's. He came to the Valley to see what Vaiden was doing with the money he had lent him.

Instead of repaying the debt, Vaiden gave Hunt the date grove he had planted. Clinton Hunt named his spread Vista Alegre (Happy View) and worked it until 1948 when he returned to New York and his former career as an engineer.

The Montoya family lived in an adobe home on the Vaiden ranch. Says Art Montoya, "Standing at the La Quinta Resort clubhouse recently, looking down to the golf course, I could see into the past - the Montoya boys, their dogs, pet goat, horses, men picking tomatoes, the packing house, fields of corn, and a family living in great content. Life in La Quinta was great."

Kids at Play

Left to right: Art Montoya, Manuel Pizano, Jim Montoya, Ben Montoya and Dick Montoya play in a cornfield on the Vaiden Ranch.

Life at the Vaiden Ranch

*Young Ben and Dick Montoya sit down as two Mexican "**Bracero**" guest workers (far left) take a break in the packing house on the Vaiden Ranch. Also pictured are Dave Melendez, Margie Montoya and Rosemary Carrillo.*

SKEE RANCH

Council member Stanley Sniff's parents arrived in the Coachella Valley in 1915. Both physicians, Drs. Dana and Emma Sniff gave up their successful medical practices to move to an inhospitable and largely barren desert where they farmed and sold dates commercially. Says Stanley Sniff, "My parents loved the beauty and promise of the desert."

In the spring of 1926, an Iowa investor, George Skee, asked Dr. Dana Sniff to oversee the creation of a date garden on 20 acres of land he owned where present-day Jefferson Street meets Avenue 52 at the Coachella Valley's first traffic circle.

Dr. Dana Sniff and his crew leveled the land and planted 1000 Deglet Noor date palm shoots.

Starting A New Grove

Dr. Dana Sniff planting date palms on the ranch, circa 1926.

Though Innovative Communities, developer of the Watermark Villas residential community, has cleared most of the palms, they have preserved a smaller date grove and placed a commemorative plaque near the clubhouse to note the history of the property and the efforts of its early pioneers.

Council Member Stanley Sniff provided the wording, which reads in part, "In 1926, pioneers like my dad and others changed the Valley through agriculture. Their efforts, under harsh and forbidding circumstances, brought a Garden of Eden reality to the Valley. Vision, determination and water made it happen."

CHAPTER TWO

The La Quinta Hotel was built in an area the Cahuilla Indians called "Happy Hollow."

Prospects for Prosperity

 The La Quinta Hotel started an influx of visitors and investors that created a neighborhood village with a club atmosphere. It wouldn't be long before the social calendar included fewer tea parties and more tee times.

"Every year, the Mecca of thousands seeking the sunshine, beauty, and dry, health-giving climate of the desert has earned La Quinta an international reputation as America's foremost desert resort community."

— *Presenting La Quinta*, brochure, 1943, Palm Springs Land and Irrigation Company

La Quinta Hotel

More legend surrounds the reasons why Walter Morgan came upon this place to build a hotel. One account says he fought on the bitter cold European front lines of World War I and vowed if he made it home alive to seek out the "driest, warmest, most enjoyable climate," Another report says Morgan was deeded title to a 1,400 acre parcel of land south of Point Happy through a federal patent from the U.S. Department of the Interior.

Whatever the impetus, once Morgan became a wealthy San Francisco aristocrat, he made good on his vow and came to La Quinta to grow alfalfa and date palms. In 1925, he commissioned the building of a secluded hacienda-style hotel by prominent architect, Gordon B. Kaufman at a cost of $150,000. The 20-room La Quinta Hotel opened its doors during the Christmas season of 1926.

Come On Down

A crowd of well-wishers, center, is on hand for the 1927 festivities. Horses gave way to fancy touring cars by 1937.

INDIO, CALIFORNIA
FRIDAY,
FEBRUARY 4, 1927

HOTEL LA QUINTA GRAND OPENING

Newest Winter Resort of Unique Style

The opening of the new Hotel La Quinta, one of the finest winter resorts in the county, took place last Saturday evening. With all the rooms reserved in advance and 125 guests for dinner, the occasion was an auspicious one.

Nothing of a formal nature was arranged, but visitors from all parts of Southern California enjoyed the dance after the dinner.

The hotel, built in the style of a Spanish hacienda, was recently completed at a cost of $150,000. Altho simple in architecture, nothing has been omitted, which will make for the comfort and well-being of guests.

The name, which translated means "the country retreat" is particularly suited to the new hotel, located in a secluded corner of the Coachella Valley, with hills for a background and a wonderful view of the desert spread out before it.

Excellent roads lead to the hotel, which is about 22½ miles from Palm Springs, 8½ miles from Indio and 2½ miles southwest of Point Happy, and occupies a portion of the 1,400-acre tract owned by the Desert Development Co., of which Mr. W. H. Morgan is president.

Even though its clientele was international, the building of the La Quinta Hotel was a local labor of love. Homesteader Manning Burkett served as chief carpenter. E.F. Woodhouse, who came up with a method for curing tamarisk wood for furniture, was in charge of the hotel's interior. Instead of importing bricks and tile, the crew built two kilns on the site where they fired adobe from local clay.

The hotel's design was a Spanish Colonial Revival style with signature details such as loggias, arches, chimneypots in many forms, dining armadas, and private enclosed patios. Twenty casitas, or free-standing cottages, dotted the lush grounds designed by Edward Huntsman-Trout.

The original 20 casitas were built in two concentric ovals around an interior courtyard, and were named alphabetically for saints: San Anselmo, San Benito, San Carlos, San Dimas, San Jacinto, San Lucas, San Marcos, San Nicolas, San Onofre, San Petro, San Quintin, San Rafael, San Sebastian, San Timoteo, and Santa Ursula.

During World War II, members of General George Patton's staff reportedly used the hotel facilities. Although troops were never officially stationed there, government signs were posted to restrict unauthorized entry.

Walter Morgan should also be credited with bringing golf to the Coachella Valley. The hotel grounds included a nine-hole golf course designed by Norman Beth and built for $50,000. It was the first golf course built in the Coachella Valley and was open to the public for a greens fee of $1.

Santa Rosa Room
This was the hotel's original lobby.

Lounging Around
Guests kept cool around the swimming pool.

INDIO, CALIFORNIA
FRIDAY, FEBRUARY 25, 1927

LA QUINTA ENTERTAINS

EXCURSION PARTY

While the S. P. trains were marooned here last week, the Raymond-Whitcomb tourists who were among the passengers, were taken out to the La Quinta Hotel for a rest and recreation. There were 55 in the party including Mr. Charles Taft, son of former president William Howard Taft.

It is reported that the party was delighted with the trip and stayed for dinner and enjoyed a social dance in the evening.

Mr. and Mrs. W. H. Crocker, of San Francisco, and members of the Crocker family of Southern Pacific fame are registered at the La Quinta Hotel.

ANNOUNCING

The opening to the public of the Golf Course in connection with the new Hotel La Quinta.

A maintenance charge of one dollar per person per day will be made as "Green Fee".

Golf clubs will be available for rental at a nominal sum.

— ALSO —
SADDLE HORSES FOR HIRE

La Mirage
At left, the hotel's original dining room, La Mirage.

Hotel Makes News

From the beginning, the publicity was buzzing. La Quinta was THE place for movie stars and the upper crust to relax in style. President Eisenhower paid a visit. During a break from filming "Jezebel," Bette Davis told a reporter, "I'm off to La Quinta."

Two Franks
Frank Capra and Frank Sinatra at the La Quinta Hotel, circa 1970s.

FRANK CAPRA'S WONDERFUL LIFE

The renowned Hollywood director Frank Capra first came to the La Quinta Hotel in 1934 to turn the short story "Night Bus" (which he read in a Palm Springs barber shop) into the script for "It Happened One Night." The film was the first to win every Oscar it was nominated for, and swept the 1934 Academy Awards. Capra took that to mean La Quinta was his lucky charm. He returned year after year to his "Shangri-La for script writing," to create "Mr. Deeds Goes to Town," "Lost Horizon, "It's A Wonderful Life," "You Can't Take It With You," "Mr. Smith Goes To Washington," and "Meet John Doe."

In 1972, Capra and his wife, Lucille, moved to La Quinta fulltime.

Lisa Vossler remembers spending time as a child with the Capras at their casita on the grounds of the La Quinta Hotel while her mother, Judy, was general manager there. One of her fondest memories is of their shared joy watching hummingbirds buzzing around the feeder on the Capra's porch. Says Lisa, "One of the most special gifts I have ever received was a snapshot of a hummingbird Frank took while I was there. I have the photo with my childhood treasures, and I can still see his sweet smile after taking the picture. What a special man he was and how lucky I was to have called him my friend, Frank."

Lucille Capra died in 1984, and Frank Capra died in 1992. They are buried side by side in the Coachella Valley Cemetery, not far from the place they loved - La Quinta. They were survived by three children - Frank Jr., Lucille and Tom.

FROM LA QUINTA HOTEL'S FIRST BROCHURE

La Quinta, meaning in Spanish "the country home," is located in Coachella Valley near Indio, California, and is easily accessible by motor car over paved roads or via the Southern Pacific Railroad, which has a station at Indio, eight miles distant. Guests arriving by train will be met at Indio by a closed car.

La Quinta offers the guest excellent accommodations in modern two and three-bedroom adobe cottages, adjacent to the main buildings of the inn, which include a lobby, large living room, refectory, dining room, indoor and outdoor breakfast rooms, and children's dining room. Garages and quarter for chauffeurs and maids are also provided. Domestic water is furnished from deep artesian wells, rated by government analysis as 99.9 percent pure and soft.

In an atmosphere of pristine desert air and sparkling California sunshine, the guest is offered a variety of entertainments, including hiking, riding, tennis, motoring, and golf on a nine hole course.

As our accommodations are limited to fifty rooms, we can receive only a restricted number of transient guests. Those desiring reservations should make them sufficiently far in advance that there will be no likelihood of being disappointed. Reservations will be received by letter, wire or telephone.

Hotel Newsletter

A newsletter, El Heraldo de La Quinta (The La Quinta Herald), was created in 1937 to look like a newspaper to generate more publicity for the hotel. Each issue ran complete with society items, staged photos and ads from local merchants.

Celebrating the 5th Anniversary of the La Quinta Historical Society

El Heraldo de La Quinta

News of the Desert

LIMITED EDITION

VOL. 1, NO. 1

L. B. NELSON, Manager

LA QUINTA, CALIFORNIA

HELEN BRADFORD, Editor

DECEMBER, 1938

GEO. HANSEN, Advertising

California's Smartest Desert Hotel Celebrates Eleventh Successful Season

LA QUINTA Hotel continues under the personal direction of Mgr. L. B. Nelson.

LA QUINTA HOTEL, known as the mecca of socialites of the world and the favorite rendezvous for those prominent in the motion picture profession, continues the 1938-39 season December 17.

This exclusive resort underwent an extensive program of improvements last season . . . chief among which was the installation of the new swimming pool, and

work has been going forward to continue adding attractions which are appealing to its distinctive clientele.

A charming desert retreat — secluded and located in a sheltered cove of the towering Santa Rosa mountains . . . La Quinta typifies the genuine spirit of the California desert.

The hotel is modern in its physical appointments, and has a lure for those who want rest and relaxation. However, there is every inducement for play . . . horses, tennis, badminton,

Individual Bungalows a favorite of La Quinta exclusive clientele.

cycling, bowling, croquet, archery and swimming . . . all to be found at this colorful oasis in the real desert.

Mr. Nelson, who has been actively associated with the most outstanding hotels and clubs of national importance, has surrounded himself with a competent organization to assist in the operation of the La Quinta Hotel. Each employee has been carefully selected on his merits and capabilities to cater to every whim of the La Quinta Hotel's distinguished clientele.

In a sheltered cove of the towering Santa Rosa mountains nestles La Quinta Hotel and Bungalows

Sign the Guest Book, Please

Hollywood's elite and the top sports luminaries of their day found refuge at the hotel. Insuring privacy was, and still is, a hallmark of the hotel's top drawer service. But, oh, if those walls could talk…

Famous Guests from Over the Years

Greta Garbo
William Powell
Joel McCrea
Katherine Hepburn
Robert Montgomery
Erroll Flynn
Eddie Cantor
Marie Dressler
Ronald Colman
Johnny Bench
Jimmy Conners
Diane Keaton
Jack Nicklaus
Arnold Palmer
Andre Agassi
Kevin Costner
Donna Mills
Johnny Carson
Jill Ireland
Robert Wagner
Pat Benatar
George Lucas
Sylvester Stallone
Clint Eastwood
Annette Bening
Oprah Winfrey

Ginger Rogers
Joan Crawford
Marlene Dietrich
Richard Widmark
Charles Boyer
Clark Gable
Merle Oberon
Joan Blondell
Leslie Howard
Tom Landry
Tracy Austin
Warren Beatty
Lee Trevino
Joe Montana
Larry Gatlin
Ali McGraw
George Peppard
Cheryl Tiegs
Charles Bronson
Jessica Lange
Elizabeth Taylor
Harrison Ford
Michael Jackson
Natalie Cole
Chuck Fairbanks
Madonna

Celebrities at the Hotel

Above, a photographer snapped one of the delightful porches at the La Quinta Hotel. Front row, left to right Mrs. Helen Braniff, Miss Lili Damita (Mrs. Errol Flynn), Miss Dolores Del Rio (Mrs. Cedric Gibbons). Back row, Manuel Reachi of Mexico, Cedric Gibbons, and Errol Flynn. At left, Carol Lombard and Clark Gable.

New Year's Eve

Actress Bette Davis, far left, watches as Heinz Hofmann and partner dance at the 1937 gala.

✻ In the Early days of the La Quinta Hotel, "Little Joe" was the mascot and was prominently displayed on many products.

Rates

One person	. . .	$15 per day
Two persons	. . .	$25 per day
Lunch or Dinner	. . . .	$2.50

All rooms with private baths and steam heat

❦

WALTER H. MORGAN, Pres.

La Quinta   Indio, California

Early Vintage
La Quinta Hotel Postcards

Come to the Village

In 1932, Harry Kiener, representing the Big Bear Land & Water Company, purchased several thousand acres of land, part of which he dubbed Rancho La Quinta. Today, the site is occupied by The Enclave custom home development. Record crops of premium Deglet Noor dates and Marsh Seedless grapefruit are said to have been produced on the ranch.

Flush with his farming prowess, Kiener subdivided 1600 acres in the cove area into a gridiron pattern of 50 x 100 foot lots connected by graded but unpaved streets. Historical texts refer to the project as Santa Carmelita Del Vale or Vale La Quinta. Names for the streets going north-south were prefaced with "Avenida," while east-west streets were called "Calle."

Kiener was also concerned about keeping his work crew together between projects, so he put his associate, Guy Maltby, in charge of a new venture - the La Quinta Milling and Lumber Company. Maltby's office and lumber yard were among the earliest commercial buildings in the village area, along with the hexagonal building that now houses the La Quinta Historical Society Museum.

The village area of La Quinta was intended to be used as a commercial district for residents of the cove subdivisions. Unlike the straight rows of residential streets in the cove, the village was laid out with angled streets around a six-sided park. Early commercial buildings followed the Spanish Colonial Revival style made popular by the La Quinta Hotel.

Julie Hirsch grew up in the apartment above the La Quinta Milling and Lumber Company in the village. She recounted the story of actor John Barrymore (Drew Barrymore's grandfather) being sent to La Quinta to "rest and recuperate" by the movie studio to which he was under contract for an upcoming movie. Barrymore was placed in the guest house behind the lumber company office, and was denied car keys or cash.

The "cold turkey" rehab Barrymore was subjected to included having his phone calls monitored. Says Hirsch, "Mr. Barrymore was a very sick man. He would beg for a ride into town, for money, or for liquor. Someone gave him a fifth of whiskey, and that was the end of the movie plans."

Harner House

Dr. Clyde and Peggy Harner built this desert bungalow, which they called Hacienda de Harner, in 1938 as their second home. They sold it in the early 1940s, when gas rationing made travel to the desert nearly impossible. The home was purchased by the Yessyian family, members of which still live there today. This painting by Long Beach artist Esther Smeed has been restored and is hanging in the Pacific Western Bank branch managed by Dr. Harner's grandson, Mark.

Post Office

La Quinta's first Post Office opened in 1930, before a permanent postage meter could be secured. A loaner was brought in, and the first items mailed from La Quinta were marked "Calexico."

La Quinta Historical Society Museum

This 1936 building has housed a water company, land development offices, and the real estate office of Frances Hack, who was instrumental in acquiring the park for the local recreation district. The building now houses the La Quinta Historical Society Museum. Artist credit: Andre Blanché, 1994.

PLANNING THE COVE

When Harry Kiener looked out at the subdivision he created in the La Quinta cove, he envisioned a new planned community to rival Palm Springs, where "weekenders" could buy fully furnished homes, complete with linens, for $2,500. Lots were sold for $500, with $25.00 down, through a telemarketing operation.

For nearly four years, Kiener, using the company name Palm Springs Land & Irrigation Company, submitted documents to the Riverside County Planning Commission's Subdivision Committee for approval to sell lots in the cove. The commissioners had frequent concerns about the water supply, waste treatment and stormwater drainage. Several maps were approved with conditions, including the piping of domestic water to the front of each lot.

The construction of homes occurred at random. The developer's sales pitch was often aimed at speculators who bought property hoping to reap a profit without turning any dirt. Records show that 95 houses were built between 1935 and 1949. World War II created a scarcity of building materials which caused higher prices that scared off buyers and lot sales plummeted.

Most early cove houses were characterized as Spanish Colonial Revival with a Pueblo influence, and were similar in size and style to the casitas at the La Quinta Hotel. Locally produced materials, such as tile from the Joe Valenzuela Roof Company, were used at both the hotel and the houses, further reinforcing the design symmetry.

Early Bungalows

Sketch from 1948 Palm Springs Land Irrigation Company brochure depicts a typical bungalow court.

Cove Then and Now

Modest desert bungalows scattered across the empty desert have long since been replaced by well-landscaped homes in a tidy neighborhood.

Join the Desert Club

"La Quinta, in our estimation, is to Palm Springs what Beverly Hills is to Los Angeles; "The Elite Part Of The Desert," and this property may be bought on terms to satisfy the most moderate pocketbook."

Palm Springs Land and Irrigation Co., 1948

Reciprocal clubs were a popular real estate investment among second home buyers in the 1930s. The practice allowed one to enjoy full membership privileges at two separate club facilities if a residence was owned at each location. Harry Kiener saw the potential of his land investment in La Quinta increase dramatically if lot sales were tied to club membership.

His inspiration was Peter Pan Woodland Club, a hunting and fishing lodge he had pioneered in Big Bear. The plan was to offer reciprocal membership between the two clubs so that members could summer in Big Bear and winter in La Quinta. By 1947, the Desert Club was being touted nationally in Fortune Magazine. Ads called La Quinta "America's most delightful desert retreat, where Winter never comes."

As a marketing brochure promised, "The ultimate in Clubdom, THE DESERT CLUB, to be erected, providing a wealth of pastimes and desert sports. Superbly appointed and ultra-modern, privately secluded in a mountain-sheltered cove, an empire of natural beauty. Recreational facilities are scheduled to include a swimming pool, tennis and badminton courts, archery range, riding stables and ring, modern equipment for sunbathing, grand lounge, dining room, coffee shop, billiard and card rooms, and landscaped patios and terraces."

Longtime La Quinta resident Julie Hirsch remembers, "When diggers got to what they expected to be the bottom of the pool, they ran into the tops of an orchard, with trees set out in even rows. Everyone who heard about it had to come and see for themselves because they could not believe it! The amount of silt deposited on top of an earlier settler's orchard was testimony to the severity of flash flooding La Quintans were subject to in the early days."

CALIFORNIA'S
La Quinta
...and the Desert Club
..WHERE WINTER NEVER COMES!

Land of Enchantment for Your Dream Home

Within a whisper of Palm Springs . . . 3 hours from Los Angeles . . . lies secluded La Quinta, California's smartest year-round desert playground. Here, in a sun-kissed setting of Nature's own incredible technicolor contrasts, is the ultra-smart Desert Club and the carefully-zoned, long-established homesite development with its alluring opportunities for investment or ideal living. For a club vacation in dungarees or dress clothes, or for building that cherished home of your dreams, golden hours really "out of this world" are yours . . . at lovely, lazy, luxurious La Quinta! Full Color Brochure on Request.

THE DESERT CLUB, LA QUINTA, CALIFORNIA

Kiener fell ill and dropped out of the project, but a pair of his enterprising salesmen took it over and built a Streamline Modern clubhouse resembling a ship with smokestacks.

In its heyday, the Desert Club was a magnet for celebrities and others who sought a less formal atmosphere than the La Quinta Hotel. Local pioneer Frances Hack was quoted as a frequent guest of the club's poker club. Hack told a newspaper reporter, "It was kind of hush-hush, but people at the Desert Club knew about it."

Through the years, the club had a series of setbacks. In the 1950s, it was damaged in a fire and completely rebuilt as a family resort. The Desert Club closed its doors in the mid 1980s, and the buildings were burned to the ground in 1989 in a practice fire for the Riverside County Fire Department. The site was deeded to the City of La Quinta to be used as a community park, which was later named for Fritz Burns.

Rupert Yessayian fondly remembers playing at The Desert Club as a child. "For a kid, it was like an amusement park, with the big swimming pool and, what seemed to us, miles of grounds to explore. The cactus garden was really impressive."

Favorite Hideaway

Actress Rita Hayworth and friend pose by the pool, circa 1940s.

The Desert Club Burns

Below, the Fire Department takes down The Desert Club in a practice burn.

At the Dedication

Dedication of the Club flagpole took place in 1939 and was conducted by the Boy Scouts and officials of the American Legion. Standing in the back row fourth from the left is Gordon Cologne who became a California Legislator.

Water & Power Fuel the Future

 Early exploration by horseback, then stagecoach, then railroad brought would-be farmers and settlers to the Coachella Valley. Water, a commodity that at first glance seemed in short supply in the desert, was readily available from an underground aquifer beneath the desert floor. Well-drillers got steady work digging down 500 feet in less than two days to bring pure, artesian water to the surface. Wells, however, were not a sustainable means of supplying water as the underground supply levels dropped and costs to extract it increased.

Unfortunately, stormwater proved to be an even greater challenge. Because of the area's topography, Point Happy and Marshall's Cove would often flood. Residents knew early on that they'd have to get organized to acquire Colorado River water for irrigation and build levees to prevent flooding. In 1918, the Coachella Valley County Water District was established. Even so, due to the Depression and World War II, it took 30 years for Colorado River water to reach the Valley.

Electricity came to the Valley in 1914, and was extended to Marshall's Cove in 1919. Power was delivered to the present-day cove area in 1932 as part of Harry Kiener's real estate development boom there. Electric services were taken over by Imperial Irrigation District in 1943.

Telephone service became available in the east Coachella Valley in 1903, when Charlie King figured out how to use the top wire of a fence along the railroad as a conduit to send local messages from downtown Indio to ranches in Coachella,

Mecca and Thermal. In 1906, a local phone company was incorporated. One of its first expenses was the purchase of nearly 1500 telephone poles salvaged from the railroad right-of-way at a cost of $1.50 each.

Multi-party lines were not uncommon. According to a published report, the phone company showed many lines as 10-party, but the actual number depended only on the "ingenuity of the operators determining new code rings to identify customers." La Quinta council member Stanley Sniff remembers party lines of up to 16 homes well into the 1950s.

La Quinta Stormwater Protective Works

Above left, Coachella Valley Water District crews work at the corner of Highway 111 and Jefferson Street to connect the La Quinta storm drain to the main drainage line ending at the Salton Sea. Above right, pictured from left are Mayor John Pena, Bob Baier, State Assemblyman William Bradley at the lectern, Father Brennen and Tom Levy, 1986.

Old Water Pipes

From left, Barbara Irwin, museum volunteer, Rick Dickhaut, CVWD finance director, and maintenance workers Horatio Domingo and Mario Gomez look at surplus WWI Navy boiler pipes used during 1930s construction in the cove.

Cotton Balls to Golf Balls

Before it became a haven of green belts and golf balls, PGA WEST was a ranch of green pastures and cotton balls. Brothers Leon and Mark Kennedy arrived in 1947. Their primary crop was cotton, but they also raised cattle, and had a feed lot where PGA WEST's Stadium Course is today. The families with six children between them farmed 2200 acres around their ranch on Jefferson Street and Avenue 56.

Leon Kennedy served as President of the Coachella Valley Water District from 1954 to 1976. The brothers were occasionally approached by people interested in buying land. Son Tom remembers mobster Moe Green from The Purple Gang in Chicago stopping by, but a deal was never consummated. The Kennedy children sold off most of the ranch after the patriarch brothers passed away in the 1970s.

By the 1980s, Landmark Land Company had acquired the La Quinta Hotel. Landmark Senior Vice President Ernie Vossler would often drive to Thermal airport to pick up VIPs arriving by private plane. He loved the location of the former Kennedy Cotton Ranch and thought it would be an ideal home for PGA tour professionals and golf lovers to practice championship play in a secluded environment all their own.

In 1984, with the City of La Quinta newly incorporated, plans were approved for PGA WEST. The Kennedy family spent considerable time and money to level the sand dunes on their property to make it suitable for farming. Ironically, Landmark spent even more money to build the dunes back up into hills, fairways, and sand traps.

Kennedy Brothers
Diversified Farmers
Indio, California

We worked for a seat at the family table

Farming has never been easy. It was tough for our father, and it has been no bed of roses for our generation either. Even as kids, we worked for the right to sit at the family table — and we still do.

Both of us were driving tractor 12 hours a day by the time we were 14 years old. Both of us ran combines at 35c an hour. Both of us graduated to a custom land leveling business, and eventually both of us saved enough money for the downpayment on some land of our own.

Those years of land leveling experience have stood us in good stead. We knew how much it cost to get raw land into production. And vantages of equipment.

It was the kind of experience that Bank of America was interested in too. Their field men know the farm deal. They are close to it. And if you have an idea that makes sense, they go along. At least they did for us.

They still do. Every pioneering program has its downs as well as its ups. But good years or bad, they've been personally interested and personally helpful ever since we started. And that's the kind of banking you have to have to make it.

Leon Kennedy Mark Kennedy

Bank of America
NATIONAL TRUST AND SAVINGS ASSOCIATION
MEMBER FEDERAL DEPOSIT INSURANCE CORPORATION

Kennedy's Cotton
Above, ad from Farm Journal magazine. Far left, aerial view of ranch. Left, this 1950 photo shows Leon Kennedy checking the cotton crop at Jefferson Street near Avenue 56.

Taking Care of Business

By 1947, Frances Hack had already enjoyed a stellar career as a movie studio talent scout. Among her discoveries was a five-year-old cherub named Shirley Temple. Upon retiring from show business, Hack and her husband settled in La Quinta, and went into real estate.

It didn't take long for Hack to get involved in her newly adopted community. In July 1950, she co-founded the La Quinta Chamber of Commerce with Walter Bowman. He became the group's first president and she the secretary. As council member Terry Henderson recounts, "In those days, the Chamber of Commerce members were the 'go to' people if you wanted to promote something in the community."

In the coming years, Hack and other Chamber members worked to build a community center and children's play area in the park. Since the City was not yet incorporated, the downtown park site was deeded to the Coachella Valley Parks and Recreation District by Harry Kiener, for use by everyone in the community. Thanks to her efforts, the park is now named after Frances Hack.

Vi and Chuck Messick moved to La Quinta in 1949. When Chuck became postmaster in 1951, the couple moved into the apartment on the 2nd floor above the La Quinta Post Office in the village. Life revolved around potluck suppers and Little League games in the park. Vi remembers a group of square-dancers using the concrete slab that was laid for the community center building as a dance floor. Roxie and Meron Yessayian moved from Los Angeles to La Quinta in 1950. Roxie became a licensed Realtor in 1956, and specialized in selling 5- and 10-acre "ranchettes."

The Famous Steps

Hollywood came to La Quinta again in 1958 during the filming of the biblical epic, "The Big Fisherman," starring Howard Keel as Simon Peter. A $4 million budget was used to create a record 5500 props from a 40 foot boat to Roman coins and reed pens. In order to manage the hundreds of extras needed daily, an assembly line was established for wardrobe, make-up and hair-dressing.

A filming location was set up at the top of the La Quinta cove, recreating an ancient village of 200 tents. The production met its share of challenges, including the occasional vapor trail in the sky from jets on military maneuvers. A heavy wind storm came through and flattened the tent city. As a photographer assigned to cover the production recalled, "The tents, and everything relating to the set, had been blown into the desert as far away as where Interstate 10 is today."

La Quinta Business Women
From left, Victoria Bailey, Louise Neeley, Roxy Yessayian, Alice Bailes Bell, Vi Messick and Rosie Funtas.

COACHELLA VALLEY REALTY COMPANY
77-885 Montezuma   La Quinta. California 92253
P.O. Box 191

FRANCES HACK
Broker   Telephone: 564-4161

Rosie and Gus Funtas arrived in the early 1950s to take over the small grocery store and café located on Calle Estado. The family of four lived behind the grocery store. Both boys, Gary and Mike, played on the Sparks Little League team. Many of the celebrities staying at the La Quinta Hotel frequented the grocery store and the café. Some rode up on horseback and tied their horses up outside.

One regular customer was the reclusive actress Greta Garbo. When she was in residence at the hotel, Garbo would don a "disguise" consisting of a long duster, dark glasses and a wide-brimmed Asian-style straw hat. The hotel did not sell cigarettes, so she walked from the hotel to the store, and always said the same thing: "A pack of Camels, please." Sometimes, she would linger in the café, and be met by a tall, handsome man who turned out to be British actor Brian Aherne.

Gus and Rosie Funtas weren't interested in alerting the media to the clandestine meetings. Instead, they got a kick out of the fact that Garbo was doing exactly what the cigarette manufacturer intended. She "walked a mile for a Camel."

Early Businesses

Above, Café La Quinta, on Calle Estado, when Alice Bailes Bell had the Marcella Press next door. Below, Roxie Yessayian opened La Quinta Real Estate in 1962. She was a charter member of the La Quinta Chamber of Commerce, and built a solid reputation for rentals and sales in the La Quinta area. The business is still family-owned and operated in the same location in the village.

La Quinta Sparks Baseball Team 1957

From left, back row- Brad (Butch) Davis, David English, Jim Vik, Dennis Hotchkiss, Fred Holly, Chuck Messick, Bo Hotchkiss and Mike Funtas. Front row, from left, Buddy Yessayian, Doug Partridge, Paul Goddard, Tom Kennedy and Gary Funtus.

La Quinta Country Club

When Chicago attorney Leonard Ettelson and a group of investors bought the La Quinta Hotel in 1958, they also bought 1000 acres of land around it to insure their investment. The hotel was not profitable on its own, but the group knew they could parlay the surrounding real estate into gold. The property was subdivided for estate-sized lots surrounding a golf course.

The club was incorporated in 1959 with 28 charter members. Bing Crosby, Bob Hope, Phil Harris, Randolph Scott and John Raitt were on hand to cut the ribbon. The following year, President Dwight D. Eisenhower was the guest of honor at the dedication of the club's 18-hole golf course. A modular building that was relocated from Eldorado Country Club in Indian Wells served as a temporary clubhouse with a pro shop, cocktail lounge, club room, and locker room. Members called it "The Shack," but they loved its simplicity and warm, friendly atmosphere.

A newspaper report said, "President Dwight D. Eisenhower topped off his desert vacation by dedicating the $500,000 La Quinta Country Club 18-hole championship course, then took an 8-iron and hit a ball 125 yards right down the middle of the fairway."

It was often rumored that President Eisenhower was looking to buy a home in La Quinta to use as his Western White House, but that never came to be. His brother, Edgar, however, met Leonard Ettelson through a mutual friend and not only bought a home in La Quinta, but served on the La Quinta Country Club board of directors from 1968 to 1972.

In 1962, a young Jack Nicklaus gained national TV exposure on the course at La Quinta. The following year, the club landed a deal to host the CBS Match Play Classic. As a result of the media exposure, membership tripled. In 1964, La Quinta Country Club joined a handful of other desert golf clubs to co-host a small tournament called the Palm Springs Golf Classic, which became the Bob Hope Chrysler Classic.

Ike Attends Opening

President Eisenhower, third from left, is assisted in the ribbon-cutting ceremony by Colonel Courtney S. Turner, club pro Dick Goeckner, George E. Allen, and Mrs. Edward J. Crowley.

La Quinta on TV

CBS Match Play Classic tournament, from left, Leonard Ettelson, Ed Crowley, Tommy Armour, Ellsworth Vines, 1963.

Pros Come to Town

From left, Jerry Barber, Jack Nicklaus, Gary Player and Gene Littler.

A new Mediterranean-style clubhouse described as a "jewel of the desert" was built in 1966. Leonard Ettelson's wife, Luela, hired noted Palm Springs designer Arthur Elrod to decorate the interior under her watchful eye. She was known to be a stickler for detail, down to the placement of each tree and shrub.

Local newspaper columnist Gloria Greer reported on the clubhouse opening, which was attended by 400 social and civic leaders, including Governor Edmund G. Brown and his wife, Bernice. Greer's column stated that, "California's First Lady, Bernice Brown, wore blue chiffon - an attractive color with her gray hair and sparkling eyes."

A lavishly appointed sitting room inside the clubhouse became known as the "No-No Room," when Mrs. Ettelson put velvet ropes around it to keep people from going inside. President Eisenhower's brother, Edgar, an active member of the club, had another room dedicated to him.

The club remained aligned with the hotel until the 1970s, when a group of members headed up by board president, George Collins, launched a successful effort to buy the clubhouse and golf course and make the club truly private. The board gambled on cutting off the revenue from outside play, but the wager paid off.

Says George Collins, "Our membership more than doubled. Good-sized contingents of members from New York and Chicago were joined by groups from Kansas City and South Dakota once we took over."

The venerable clubhouse that had served the club well was razed in 2005. Says club president, Joe Kirby, "In May of 2006, the membership voted to build a new 37,000 square foot clubhouse and subsequently limited membership to increase the exclusivity that many prospective members want. Our history of the past 50 years provided a foundation for our exciting future."

Bird's Eye View

Above, a 1960s aerial view shows La Quinta Country Club.

Clubhouse Rules

The rendering, below, shows how the old clubhouse, center, will be replaced in 2009.

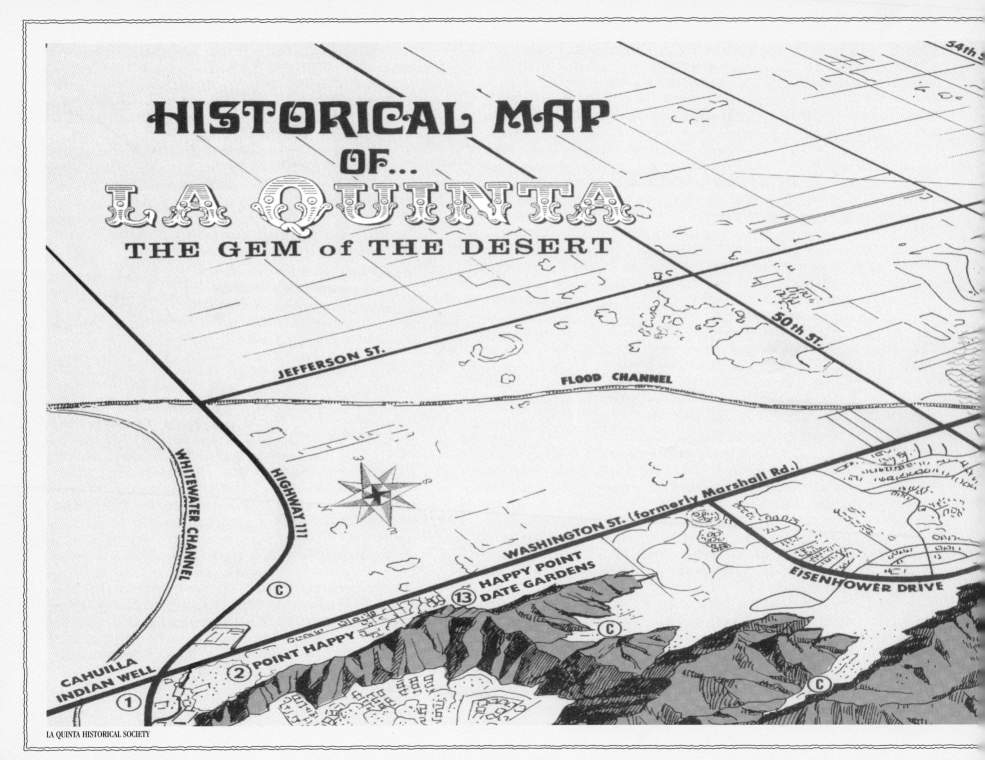

HISTORICAL MAP
OF...
LA QUINTA
THE GEM of THE DESERT

54th ST.

50th ST.

JEFFERSON ST.

FLOOD CHANNEL

WHITEWATER CHANNEL

HIGHWAY 111

WASHINGTON ST. (formerly Marshall Rd.)

EISENHOWER DRIVE

HAPPY POINT
DATE GARDENS

13

POINT HAPPY

CAHUILLA
INDIAN WELL

1

2

C

C

C

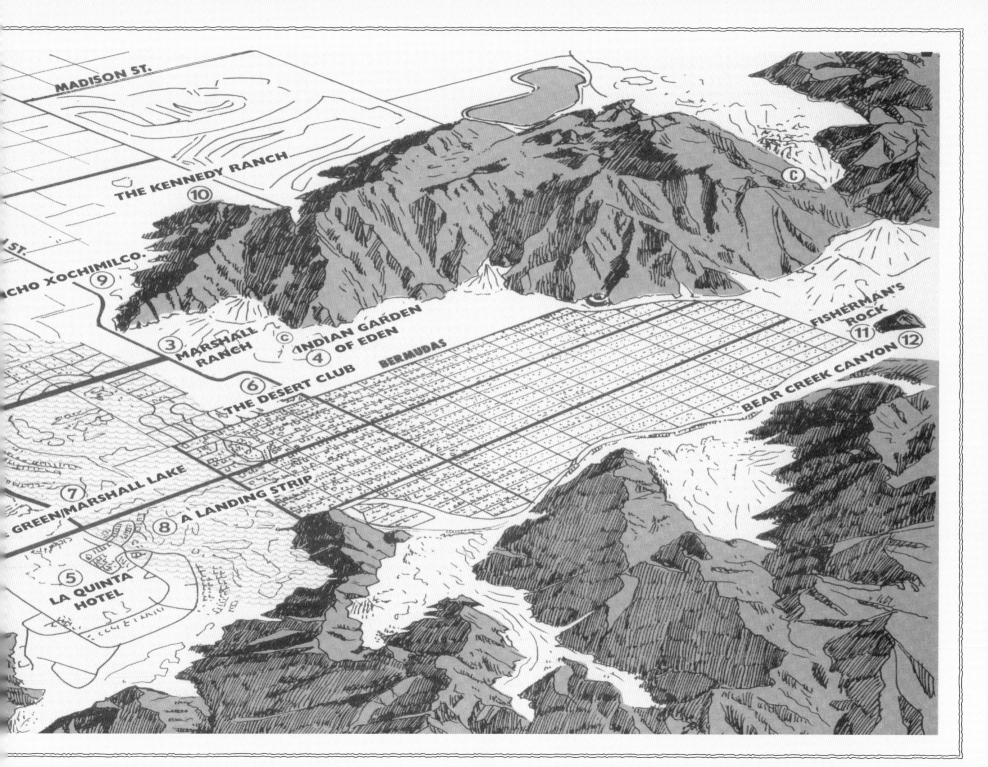

MADISON ST.

THE KENNEDY RANCH

⑩

CHO XOCHIMILCO.

⑨

⑤ MARSHALL
RANCH

ⓒ INDIAN GARDEN
OF EDEN

④

⑥
THE DESERT CLUB   BERMUDAS

FISHERMAN'S
ROCK

⑪

⑫

BEAR CREEK CANYON

⑦
GREEN/MARSHALL LAKE

⑧ A LANDING STRIP

⑤
LA QUINTA
HOTEL

ⓒ

CHAPTER THREE

A 1932 photo shows Mr. and Mrs. Hunt standing at Highway 111 and Marshall Road (now Washington Street).

The Drive to Incorporation

 From Cahuilla homeland to celebrity hideout to sportsmen's holiday, La Quinta was ready to establish itself as a city to reap rewards from the bounty it had long sowed.

And why not? A mid-century era *Sunset Magazine* called La Quinta "the essence" of the Coachella Valley.

When the 1960s brought golf to a national TV audience, La Quinta's star power rose to a new level. In 1984, PGA WEST established La Quinta as "The Western Home of Golf in America." In 2003, the *Robb Report* sealed the deal by pegging La Quinta as "America's Ultimate Golf Destination" in its Best Places to Live issue.

Hearth and Home

Economic factors brought on by World War II took a toll on La Quinta's fledgling resort industry, effectively stalling most commercial development until the late 1970s and early 1980s. In the meantime, the residents of La Quinta set about making their community a fine place to live. A real estate brochure touted La Quinta as "Suburbia at its Finest, Superb Vacationland, and a Retirement Idyll."

By 1960, the Chamber of Commerce was already referring to La Quinta as the "Gem of the Desert." They raised money to build the Community Center building in Frances Hack Park, and collected dues of $5 from each property owner to fund other civic improvements. A 1962 newsletter reports membership of 600 property owners in the Chamber of Commerce.

The La Quinta Fire and Rescue Unit, a volunteer fire department, supported community events and kept residents safe. The La Quinta Sports and Youth Center ran baseball games and other fun activities in the park. Five of the Chamber of Commerce presidents during the first 10 years of the organization were affiliated with the military.

In 1961, Avenida Serra officially became Eisenhower Drive in honor of President Dwight (Ike) Eisenhower, who was a frequent guest at the La Quinta home of Washington financier George Allen. Then Fourth District County Supervisor George Berkey observed that Ike could travel his namesake street whenever he came to play golf at La Quinta Country Club. The action was in keeping with the previous naming of all the major north-south roadways between Coachella and La Quinta after former presidents.

La Quinta Neighborhood

Lake Cahuilla

Ancient Lake Cahuilla is long gone. But, modern Lake Cahuilla was created in 1969 as a reservoir at the end of the Coachella branch of the All American Canal. The 710-acre park, accessible off Avenue 58 and Madison Street, is operated by Riverside County, and includes a 135-acre lake stocked with bass, catfish and trout.

The Fire Belles

The La Quinta Fire Belles Chapter of the Women's Emergency Medical and Support Unit of the Volunteer Fire Department was a non-profit auxiliary dedicated to supporting and improving the volunteer fire department and its fire equipment, circa 1980.

Boosters Beat The Drum

Among the seasonal visitors and retirees enjoying La Quinta in the 1970s were two men destined to play a major role in the city's future - Fred Rice and Fred Wolff. Fred and Dottie Rice moved to La Quinta in 1974 after his career as an animator for Walt Disney Studios. Fred Wolff first came to La Quinta after World War II when his father built a small house near the top of the cove. He and wife Kay spent time at the home throughout the '70s before moving to the community permanently in 1980.

In the mid-1970s, 18 golf courses were built in the Coachella Valley, fueling a condominium bonanza. Lots in La Quinta's cove became popular for their relative affordability. Their small size (50 feet x 100 feet) made asking prices in the $4,000 range especially attractive. The cove was still somewhat rural and under-regulated when it came to code enforcement. Boosters tried three times to incorporate as a City, but the lack of an adequate tax base to pay for services made the plan impractical.

Bob and Dolly Cunard arrived in La Quinta in 1974. They moved into a 1930s estate property in the village that had belonged to noted photographer Mary Mead Maddick, whose work was featured on the covers of *Time*, *Life*, and *Redbook*. In 1981, they invested in a local watering hole called Freddy's Sandbar on Calle Tampico. The homey neighborhood hangout was, and still is, a favorite with locals.

By 1986, the Cunards had transformed their home into an intimate gourmet restaurant. To get there, Bob Cunard remembers fighting to have the property re-zoned, and enlisting the help of several environmental groups to prevent the removal of his mature trees. Cunard's was named one of the top 25 restaurants in the country, and often played host to celebrities like Clint Eastwood, Gerald and Betty Ford, Arnold

Frances Hack Ceremony

From left, Council Member Stanley Sniff, Council Member Dale Bohnenberger, Council Member Larry Allen, Frances Hack, Council Member John Pena and Mayor William Hoyle, circa 1986.

Schwarzenegger, Glen Campbell, Gene Wilder, and Arnold Palmer. Today, The Sandbar parking lot is often packed with Rolls Royces and Bentleys.

YOUTHFUL AMBITION

The Boys & Girls Club of Coachella Valley began offering satellite programs at the Community Center in Frances Hack Park in the La Quinta village in 1990. After a successful capital campaign, a new 24,000-square-foot building was opened in July of 1994 on Park Avenue off Avenue 50.

The center calls itself "The Positive Place for All," and offers daily social and athletic activities for pre-teens and teens, as well as homework assistance, and access to computers.

La Quinta Tropics/Sandbar

Boys & Girls Club of Coachella Valley

From left, John Pena, young girl, President Gerald R. Ford, Council Member Stanley Sniff, Gail Glass, Kristy Franklin, young boy, Howard & Ardith Marguleas and Council Member William (Doc) Rushworth, circa 1992.

Opportunity Knocks

In October of 1978, then-president of the Chamber of Commerce Fred Rice wrote: "1978 will be long remembered as the year the sleeping giant awoke. La Quinta is no longer the quiet, serene little cove community tucked away in the Santa Rosa Mountains. Everywhere you look - on every street from Tampico to Tecate - you can see new homes, new apartments, new faces…and new problems.

The object of the La Quinta Chamber of Commerce is to promote the civic, economic, and social welfare of the people of La Quinta. That simply means the Chamber protects all of our interests such as zoning, security, streets and roads, public safety, sports and youth activities, water quality, flood control, phone service, community clean-up, mail service, and whatever. Attend our meetings and become involved. Maybe we can solve some of your concerns and just maybe you have a solution to ours. Let's keep La Quinta something special."

One year later, a newly invigorated La Quinta Property Owners Association worked to insure that Eisenhower Drive would not be closed. With a variety of issues at hand, the Chamber and the Property Owners Association banded together to explore incorporation once more. In August of 1980, a task force

Fred Rice

was spearheaded by Fred and Kay Wolff, former government employees used to doing research and navigating the complexities of civic proceedings.

It became clear to the group that the key to succeeding with cityhood was retaining future revenue from the "four corners" intersection of Highway 111 and Washington Street. A shopping center anchored by a Von's supermarket on one corner and an auto dealership on the opposite corner were already in the works. Neighboring cities were eyeing the commercial corridor for annexation.

It was now or never for La Quinta to make its bid.

In little more than a year, petitions were drafted, signatures were gathered, and an in-depth feasibility study was written - all without paid consultants. When all was said and done, the decision rested with the Local Agency Formation Commission (LAFCO) in Riverside. Prospects did not look good. LAFCO staff was against the volunteer-drafted proposal.

Four Corners

Von's Supermarket on one corner of Highway 111 and Washington, opposite the auto dealership, 1982.

First Mayor

La Quinta's first Mayor Fred Wolff and wife Kay celebrating.

The Ayes Have It

Two busloads of residents from La Quinta made the trip to downtown Riverside on November 12, 1981 to voice support for their application.

The commission voted unanimously to support La Quinta for cityhood. In the spring of 1982, voters approved the move to cityhood with a 75% margin.

The new City of La Quinta received an overwhelming mandate of support from voters during the April 13 election, and celebrated Inauguration Day on May1, 1982. At

Voice of the Valley

Daily News

It's Wednesday, April 14, 1982

20 CENTS

24 PAGES

INDIO, CALIFORNIA

71ST YEAR — No. 34

La Quinta: Yes to cityhood

Wolff leads council balloting; ... is elected

Mayors welcome new city

LA QUINTA — The mayors of Indian Wells, Palm Desert and Indio today offered congratulations to the organizers of the successful La Quinta cityhood campaign, offering their help and urging the new city to join with them in the Coachella Valley Association of Governments.

Mayor Roger Harlow of Indio, who has been an early supporter of La Quinta's incorporation, said he nevertheless had some misgivings over the revenues that will be needed to support city services in the 20 square mile city to Indio's west.

MAYOR ROY Wilson, of Palm Desert said the incorporation timing was good and that the revenue from proposed businesses on the Highway 111 and Washington Street intersection should help make financing of the new city easier.

How they voted

INCORPORATION

Yes	1,024
No	342

COUNCIL SELECTION

At-Large	740
District	543

CITY COUNCIL

Fred Wolff	700
Dr. Eugene Abbott	570
Bob Baier	549
John Henderson	490
Judith Cox	470
Larry Allen	463
John Ryan	421
Rupert Yessayian	396
Charles Drinkworth	345
Ron Miller	340
John Klimkiewicz	313
James Wittse	202
William Martin	243
James Edwards	140

— Daily News Photos by Frank Orlando

WINNING COUNCIL CANDIDATES BOB BAIER AND FRED WOLFF CONGRATULATE EACH OTHER

that time, the oath of office was administered to five council members - Eugene Abbott, Robert Baier, Judith Cox, John Henderson and Fred Wolff.

A wide range of ordinances were passed in the first few months including mandatory trash pick-up, penalties for illegal dumping, a leash law and stricter residential building standards that dictated minimum house and room sizes, landscaping and architectural design.

THE OFFICIAL CITY OF LA QUINTA INAUGURATION DAY CEREMONY
MAY 1, 1982
THE LA QUINTA HOTEL

HONORARY CHAIRPERSONS
Frances Hack Frank Capra

INAUGURATION DAY COMMITTEE

Eugene Abbott	Paul Goetcheus	Tom Thornburgh
Robert Baier	Bernard Gordon	Patricia Reilly
Mike Brown	Bea Johnson	Bob Yessayian
Lawrence Cunningham	Trish Klimkiewicz	Don Zaraski
Ray Dee	Beverly Montgomery	

HOSTESSES

Ruby Dale	Vi Messick	Marie Seaman
Natalie Forbes	Didi Miguel	Angela Stanley
Bea Johnson	Beverly Montgomery	Felicia Simonson
Jean Klein	Marjane Moore	Lee Thomas
Trish Klimkiewicz	Dottie Rice	Vera Thaxton
Kate Lester	Josephine Riesner	Naomi Willoughby
Betty Mazza	Danice Ryan	Roxie Yessayian

INAUGURATION DAY SPONSORS
The La Quinta Hotel   The Desert Club of La Quinta
Palm Springs Savings and Loan

INAUGURATION DAY CONTRIBUTORS

Mr. M. C. Brennan   Col. and Mrs. Sherman A. Smith, USMC (Ret.)
Mr. and Mrs. Paul Goetcheus   Myrl and Kenneth Weise
Alice and Alfred Martin   Naomi and Roscoe Willoughby
Mr. E. George Marzicola

DONATIONS

The La Quinta Youth and Sports Center gratefully acknowledges the gift of $1000 from Landmark Land, Inc., Mr. Ernest Vossler, Senior Vice President.

The City of La Quinta gratefully acknowledges the gift of $500 from Mr. Jim Wiltse, owner of La Quinta Circle K Store.

The people of La Quinta wish to express their appreciation for the gift of the United States and California flags and the Mayor's gavel from Mr. and Mrs. Carol W. Jones of the La Quinta Country Club.

Transportation for the Mayor is provided by Country Club International Limousines, Tina Miller, President.

LA QUINTA TASK FORCE FOR INCORPORATION
MEMBERS

Eugene Abbott	Dena Corlett	Marie and Roger Horton
Larry Allen	Larry Cunningham	Jean and Chuck Howe
Bob Baier	Georgia and Frank Demarbies	Johnny Johnson
Ray Barker	Muriel Dickey	Tom Kelso
Martin Beck	Paul Goetcheus	Jean and Bert Klein
Maurice Beidler	John Henderson	Pat and John Klimkiewicz
Sylvia and Wilfred Lawson	Stacey Paxton	Freda Terry
Betty Mama	Pat Reilly	Ken Weise
Margaret Miele	Dottie and Fred Rice	Polly and Peter Weitzman
Dale Miles	Danice and John Ryan	Naomi Willoughby
Beverly and Jim Montgomery	Marie Seaman	Kay and Fred Wolff
Carol and Dave Parkinson	Angela Stanley	Jan and Jock Urquhart
	Roxie Yessayian	

CONTRIBUTING ORGANIZATIONS

Coachella Valley Realty	La Quinta Liquor
Country Club	La Quinta Property Owners
International Limousines	Lawrence Inc.–Italo's Restaurant
La Quinta Chamber of Commerce	Miele & Miele Inc.
La Quinta Hotel	Simon Motors

INDIVIDUAL DONATIONS

Dr. Eugene Abbott	Margaret Miele
Frances Hack	Martin Stone
Roger Horton	Peter Weitzman
Bert Klein	

The City of La Quinta wishes to express its appreciation to those who gave generously for the numerous donations under $100.

THE LA QUINTA CITYHOOD INAUGURATION AND INTRODUCTION OF THE CITY COUNCIL CEREMONY

INVOCATION	The Reverend Don Johnson, Pastor, Family Heritage Church
NATIONAL ANTHEM	Sung by: Daphne Payne Lewis Accompanist: Gil Quesada
INTRODUCTIONS	Mr. Gary Wiedle, Executive Director Coachella Valley Association of Governments
GREETINGS	The Honorable Edmund G. (Pat) Brown, Former Governor of California
ELECTION RESULTS	Mr. Robert Fitch, Chief Administrative Officer, County of Riverside
PRESENTATION OF GAVEL	The Honorable Alfred A. McCandless Supervisor, Fourth District, County of Riverside
MAYOR'S ADDRESS	The Honorable Fred Wolff, Mayor, City of La Quinta
PRESENTATION OF RESOLUTIONS	The Members of the La Quinta City Council Mrs. Judith Cox Mr. John Henderson Mr. Robert Baier Dr. Eugene Abbott Mr. Fred Wolff
THE LORD'S PRAYER	Sung by: Mrs. Donna Andrews
BENEDICTION	The Reverend Peter Brennan, Pastor, St. Francis of Assisi Catholic Church

You are asked to rise for the Invocation and remain standing for the singing of the National Anthem. Please stand also for the Benediction.

After the officials have been escorted off the platform, you are invited to meet with them and join in refreshments.

Guests are invited to tour the grounds of the La Quinta Hotel.

Cover: City Seal
Designed by FRED RICE
Adopted May 1, 1982

Roll Up Your Sleeves

 Along with the decision whether or not to incorporate, voters were asked to choose a city council (in the event the incorporation passed). Task force leader, Fred Wolff, obtained the most votes and was chosen by his fellow council members to be mayor. The only woman who stood for election, Judith Cox, was also elected, in spite of the fact she ran in opposition to incorporation.

Says Cox, "I ran for Council because everyone seemed caught up in the idea of becoming a City and I just wanted to make sure someone was asking the tough questions." She remembers feeling somewhat overwhelmed by her own victory, and recalls the best piece of advice she got early on from a representative of the California League of Cities who said, " 'Honorable' is a reminder, not a description. Never forget you are a public servant."

While support from the community was ample, operating funds were scarce. Two small offices were rented on Calle Estado to serve as City Hall. Meetings were held in the Community Center nearby. When it came time to hire a City Manager, it was not clear how their sole employee would be paid.

A handful of qualified applicants were interviewed, including a bearded, former Peace Corps worker named Frank Usher. Unfazed by the shoestring budget and herculean task of starting a City from scratch, Usher was hired, and proved to be adept at bringing much-needed resources together.

One of the earliest private sector partners to come to the table was Landmark Land Company. Landmark leveraged its credit to help the City Council get a bond issue to improve La Quinta infrastructure. In exchange for vacating Jefferson Street south of Avenue 54 so they could build PGA WEST, Landmark pledged $1 million to community projects.

"We were blessed," says Judith Cox. "People like Ernie Vossler from Landmark wanted to see La Quinta thrive and they did things from the heart."

City Council

From left, Council Member Dale Bohnenberger, Council Member John Pena, Council Member William Hoyle, Mayor Judith Cox and Council Member Stanley Sniff, 1984.

First Four Mayors

From left, third Mayor Larry Allen, second Mayor Bob Baier, fourth Mayor Judith Cox, first Mayor Fred Wolff and Council Member John Henderson (Terry Henderson's son), circa 1985.

A Clean Slate

Because La Quinta was only sparsely developed at the time of incorporation, City and Chamber of Commerce leaders believed they had a unique opportunity to create an image and build a thriving community around it. Mayor Fred Wolff put it this way - "The new city of La Quinta is very fortunate. (It) has a choice of what it wants to be."

Proponents went to work to determine how to capture the past, capitalize on the present and plan for the future. They quickly identified several "wants" and "needs" ranging from the philosophical pursuit of intellectual diversity to the installation of flood control measures to protect lives and property. Fred Rice put his considerable artistic talents to work designing logos and seals - first for the newly incorporated City, and later for the Chamber of Commerce, Rotary Club, Historical Society, La Quinta On Stage and St Francis Church.

While determined locals laid out their agendas for progress, the world continued to

The Western home of American golf.

PGA WEST Resort Homes by Sunrise. Jefferson & 54th, La Quinta.

GRAND OPENING–AUGUST 31st

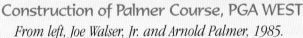

Construction of Palmer Course, PGA WEST

From left, Joe Walser, Jr. and Arnold Palmer, 1985.

beat a path to La Quinta's door for world-class golf and tennis. By this time, Landmark Land Company owned the La Quinta Hotel Golf & Tennis Resort. The tennis center and stadium they built next to the venerable hotel property hosted a number of national championships, and attracted the world's top professionals.

But it was golf that dominated the energies of Landmark senior vice presidents Ernie Vossler and Joe Walser, Jr., both veteran PGA Tour members. In order to add a golf course to the resort, two million cubic yards of dirt were moved, 20 acres of lakes were put in place and 3,000 date palm trees were planted.

Building of the Stadium Course

PGA WEST of America Course Opens

From left, Pat Rielly, Andy Vossler, Ernie Vossler, Joe Walser, Jr., Steve Walser and Deane Beman, January 1986.

Landmark for La Quinta

No one knows the mystic of the La Quinta Hotel better than former general manager Judy Vossler. Even today, the allure of the storied hotel property captivates anyone who sets foot on the lush grounds. While certain things have changed, all of the enchantment remains.

Judy Vossler shares these thoughts:

"When Walter Morgan established La Quinta Hotel, one of his goals was to build a secluded place where his Hollywood friends could relax and enjoy privacy. I think Frank Capra should be credited for leading the way for many of the celebrities to La Quinta Hotel. Through the decades, anyone who is 'anybody' has found the way to La Quinta Hotel.

"I was in management at La Quinta Hotel from 1980 through 1993, for a decade I was proud to be the general manager of what was considered to be the best and most special resort hotel in the Coachella Valley. When I arrived in 1980, La Quinta Hotel was a winter season hotel with 76 rooms, one pool and no golf or tennis. Most of the employees lived on property during the months the hotel was open. That created a family atmosphere which shaped my management style.

"When the City of La Quinta incorporated, La Quinta Hotel was certainly the largest business in town. Our company, Landmark, recognized that it was incumbent on us to help grow the community wisely through community spirit that would support smart growth. One of the ways we accomplished that was through community activities that were open and affordable to the public such as La Quinta Historical Society gatherings and Halloween, Christmas, New Years, Easter and 4th of July events.

"Landmark was dedicated to accommodating the guests with style and grace, taking care of our staff members and contributing to and growing the newly incorporated City of La Quinta. La Quinta Hotel grew in phases during my tenure. By 1993, we could boast being the second largest hotel in the Palm Springs valley with 650 rooms, challenging golf, exceptional tennis facilities and a staff of over 1,000 whose goal was to preserve the history and reputation of La Quinta Hotel. In hindsight, I believe expanding in phases

Joe Walser, Jr. and Ernie Vossler

Walter Morgan Residence

Dedication of Renker Pool

Fred Renker, La Quinta Hotel's first tennis pro, with hotel general manager, Judy Vossler, at the ceremony dedicating the pool in his honor.

was key to maintaining the feel of charm and quaintness of La Quinta Hotel that remains today.

"The hotel's reputation as a very special place has enticed many celebrities to enjoy themselves. And, they've all been here from early Hollywood icons such as Gable and Garbo to today's rock stars, sports celebrities and top business magnates. As Capra lured the early motion picture stars to La Quinta Hotel, it was probably Robert Wagner, Natalie Wood and Stephanie Powers who brought the television generation with the filming in La Quinta of the pilot of the long-running Hart to Hart TV series.

La Quinta Tennis Club

From left, Johnny Carson, Charlie Pasarell and Jackie Cooper, circa 1985.

"Landmark knows we accomplished the mission of integrating a resort hotel full of out of town visitors with local residents because so many adults today tell us about their memories of various activities they attended annually at La Quinta Hotel."

HOTEL HIGHLIGHTS

During Prohibition, guests arrange to meet in the hotel's Santa Rosa Lounge for their nightly "Orange Blossom Special." The waiters serve fresh squeezed orange juice, into which the guests casually pour their choice of spirits from hidden silver flasks.

In 1927, a nine-hole golf course opens at the hotel with greens fees of $1. The hotel adds six tennis courts and a pro shop in 1937.

In 1953, Ginger Rogers marries Jacques Bergerac on the grounds of the hotel. A few years later, when the hotel is sold to Leonard Ettelson, his wife requests that the entire structure be painted pink.

In 1988, the hotel begins a $45 million expansion that creates a 17,000-square-foot ballroom along with two new restaurants and a dramatic outdoor central plaza.

In 1993 La Quinta Hotel Golf & Tennis Club officially becomes La Quinta Resort & Club. Five years later, the resort adds a 23,000-square-foot spa.

In the last two years, the resort has continued to upgrade guest rooms and common areas to keep up with technology but maintain that special sense of place. Even at 80 years old, the La Quinta Resort & Club is considered a trendsetter as one of the world's finest resorts.

In 2006, the resort became part of Hilton Hospitality Inc.'s Waldorf-Astoria Collection luxury brand.

La Quinta Tennis Club

Celebrity tournaments held each year.

Robert Wagner

You Gotta Have Art

 Since other Valley communities were also drawing visitors with golf and tennis, La Quinta sought another image for their special place. Like the native Cahuilla and enterprising real estate tycoons of the 1930s, City leaders saw the village at the foot of the cove as the heart of La Quinta.

A proposal was written, based on an idea by then Chamber of Commerce President, John Klimkiewicz, to establish a cultural and arts center located between the Community Center, the Desert Club and the La Quinta Hotel. A retail village would have a pedestrian-friendly ambiance similar to Carmel or Laguna Beach, with art galleries, book stores and coffeehouses.

The central park and Community Center seemed like a natural place to hold a significant annual arts festival to promote their venture and bring in visitors and working artists. The La Quinta Arts Foundation was incorporated in February of 1983. They had the will, now they just needed a way to finance their vision.

At the suggestion of Tom Thornburg, owner of the Desert Club and a member of the City Planning Commission, a group of influential businessmen was convened at the Desert Club. They included Ernie Vossler from Landmark Land Company, Fred Simon of Simon Motors, Bill Burnett, developer of Plaza La Quinta Shopping Center, George Marzicola, developer of Washington Square, and Merv Johnson, developer of Laguna de la Paz.

The idea was presented and "the ask" was made for $5,000 from each one. Either on the spot or shortly thereafter, every one of them pitched in, and a few others followed.

25th Anniversary
The 25th anniversary poster for the La Quinta Arts Festival

Weidenhamer Recreates Marshall Road

Dale Kirkpatrick, President of Bank of the Desert, commissioned artist John Weidenhamer to create a painting of Marshall Road (Washington Street) from an old black and white photo given to the artist by Fred Rice. The artwork was made into a commemorative poster distributed by Bank of the Desert in 1987.

A Festival Is Born

The inaugural festival was held at the Desert Club in March of 1983 with comedian and artist Red Skelton as the honorary chairman. The effort was pulled off almost entirely by volunteers. The only professional in the group was then executive director Barbara Barnett, who was recruited from the Sawdust Festival in Laguna. Fifty juried artists exhibited and thousands of people came to stroll the grounds.

By the late 1980s, attendance was approaching 15,000 and art sales were close to $350,000. Each year since then, the festival has grown to become one of the top fine art festivals in the country. Two artists - Zeny Cieslikowski and John Wiedenhamer - have exhibited in every show since the beginning. A total of 2,027 artists have been a part of the festival.

The original goal of the La Quinta Arts Foundation to promote the city as a haven for artists has certainly come to pass. According to Foundation Executive Director, Christi Salamone, "Dozens of artists have moved to La Quinta as a result of their participation in the festival. In fact, we're seeing the results of our efforts come full circle as we present scholarships to local students and find them returning to the community after college to participate in the La Quinta arts scene."

Merv Griffin and Ava Gabor
Admiring a sculpture at the festival.

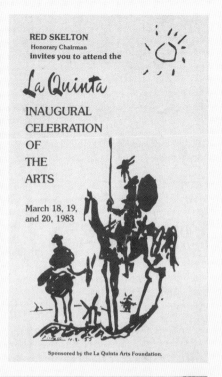

RED SKELTON
Honorary Chairman
invites you to attend the

La Quinta

INAUGURAL
CELEBRATION
OF
THE
ARTS

March 18, 19,
and 20, 1983

Sponsored by the La Quinta Arts Foundation.

This Corner of the Desert ◦ Snake Jagger

LA QUINTA ARTS FESTIVAL
March 16, 17, 18, 19, 1995 ◦ La Quinta, California

Festival Poster by Snake Jagger

Innagural Festival, Desert Club, March 1983

A Dream Becomes Reality

In the early 1970s, the Commission for the Bishop of America sent Father Raymond Bluett to Italy to serve as spiritual advisor to movie director Franco Zeffirelli for his film "Brother Sun, Sister Moon," depicting the life of St. Francis of Assisi. As production on the film wrapped up, the two men watched with sadness as a replica of the original San Damiano church of St. Francis was dismantled.

The two vowed that someday, somewhere, they would build a church of stone, wood and tile as a testimony to the beauty of their faith. Father Bluett became weary of traveling and was assigned to the Indian Wells parish. The growing congregation met wherever they could for Sunday Mass, caravanning from the La Quinta Community Center, to Crocker Bank in Indian Wells, and Simon Motors Cadillac dealership on Highway 111.

When it came time to build their own place of worship, Franco Zeffirelli said, "It seems that God is asking us to fulfill that vow." Architect Robert Ricciardi drew the plans for a basilica-style church of Romanesque design that, he said, "is meant to lift your soul to heaven."

Ill health forced Father Bluett to retire in 1982 and the parish was assigned to Reverend Peter Brennan. Alice Bayles was a reporter for the *Palm Desert Post* and filed a story that read, "Upon the broad shoulders of this genial Irishman rested the monumental task of fulfilling another person's dream, the completion of a church modeled after one St. Francis built with his own hands over seven centuries ago." Funds were raised and St. Francis of Assisi church in La Quinta held its first mass on Holy Thursday in 1984.

Saint Francis continues to experience dramatic growth in attendance as the parish's population swells. The church has over 3,000 registered families, and projections show that 4,000 new parishioners could join in the next five years.

Says Saint Francis financial coordinator, Tom Ward, "Saint Francis has a proud history in La Quinta, and looks forward to the anticipated growth in our membership and our ministry. We're here to serve the community for generations to come."

Artist At Work
Polish-born muralist Alexander Rosenfield.

CHURCH HIGHLIGHTS

The 16 murals that cover the alcoves of the sanctuary are recreations of frescoes by Renaissance artist Giotto in the mother church in Assisi, Italy. The faithful recreations were painted by La Quinta artist Alexander Rosenfeld, using water-soluble acrylic to discourage fading. Rosenfeld was 82 when he did the murals, working nine hours each day, six days a week for two and a half years.

The sanctuary crucifix depicting Christ and St. Francis was carved from a single piece of pepperwood (except for Christ's extended arms) by sculptor Ivo Demetiz of Ortesi, Italy. It is the only one of its kind.

The altar of sacrifice and the pulpit, also designed by an Italian artist, depicts St. Francis with St. Clare of Assisi - founder of the poor Clares - one of the first known altars to honor a woman saint.

The wrought iron chandeliers were crafted by La Quinta artisan Dino Estrada, duplicating the original design at a fraction of the cost of importing the fixtures from Italy.

The stained glass windows were crafted in Ireland and set into place by Irish installers from the fabricator.

The Van Zoeren pipe organ has 4,000 pipes that were individually handcrafted in Europe and casework of solid American white oak, stained in walnut to match the décor.

Preserving History

Alice Bailes Bell chronicled the goings-on in La Quinta as a reporter for the Palm Desert Post newspaper. She was also the proprietor of the Marcella Press, a small publishing company that produced "mini-biographies of the 'near famous' and retirees." Her offices were on Calle Estado, down the street from City Hall, in one of the oldest commercial buildings in La Quinta.

So, when then-Mayor Larry Allen approached her in 1984 to ask her to organize a Historical Society for La Quinta, the idea clicked. Articles of Incorporation were filed in 1985. Judy Vossler, then manager of the La Quinta Hotel, donated the $45 for the recording fee.

The first board of directors consisted of: Alice Bailes, president; Celia Griffes, vice president; Michael Mendoza, treasurer; Pat Jiles, secretary; Robert Pierce, curator; Janiel Esmeralda, research; Verle Vines, membership; Fred Rice, publicity; Bob Griffes, land development; Dru Pierce, family albums & tapes; Judy Vossler, consultant.

Fred Rice followed Bailes Bell as president, and became known as La Quinta's official historian. He proved to be a wealth of information about La Quinta as a haven for celebrities, and he was an avid researcher of local Indian history.

Patrons are continually amazed by the amount of history that's captured in the petite museum in the center of the La Quinta village. By 2008, a $2.5 million expansion will transform the bungalow into a 8,000-square-foot interactive showplace. New features are set to include electronic and hands-on exhibits, computer stations, classrooms, a gift shop, and kitchen facilities.

Says Historical Society President Donald Arends, "Our new space will allow us to collaborate with other area museums and share rotating exhibits of local interest."

Historical Society
Hal Linden and Historical Society President Ned Mills, circa 1996.

Proclamation
Council Member Terry Henderson presents proclamation to Alice Bailes Bell for years of service with the Historical Society, circa 1998.

Historical Society Christmas Lunch
Standing (from left), Louise Neeley, Cindy Mills and Pat Cross. Sitting (from left), Barbara Good, Shirley Coffee and Audrey Miline.

CHAPTER FOUR

The La Quinta Cove neighborhood is surrounded by hiking trails that wind their way into the surrounding mountains.

The Community
Comes Together

PHOTOGRAPHER MARK STEPHENSON

 Long before he was mayor of La Quinta, a young Don Adolph worked in the Los Angeles architecture firm of land developer Fritz Burns. Mayor Adolph remembers Burns was a deal maker of Donald Trump proportions, who owned construction projects throughout Southern California, the Bay Area and Hawaii.

For most of the 1960s, Burns acquired land in La Quinta until he was estimated to have controlled some 4,000 acres worth $10 million. In 1972, Fritz Burns bought the Desert Club and promptly erected a sign that read, "Welcome to La Quinta - home of the next Saks Fifth Avenue." While the high-end retailer has yet to open a La Quinta store, there is a city park named after Fritz Burns.

Going for the Green

Professional golfers and PGA Tour members, Ernie Vossler and Joe Walser, Jr., first started eyeing property in the Coachella Valley for master plan golf community development while they were in the desert to play in the Palm Springs Golf Classic in the early 1960s, prior to the tournament becoming the Bob Hope Chrysler Classic.

In the early 1970s, these two partners established Landmark Land Company, Inc. in La Quinta and began development of La Quinta Hotel Golf & Tennis Resort with the first undertaking being the world-renowned Pete Dye Mountain Course. Next was Landmark's acquisition of prized real estate on which they created PGA WEST.

PGA WEST®

PGA WEST encompasses 2,010 acres, recreational facilities and six championship golf courses with home building begun in the mid-1980s by well known local developer-builder Sunrise Company. Signature golf course designs have been created by Pete Dye, Jack Nicklaus, Greg Norman, Arnold Palmer and Tom Weiskopf. Membership pre-sales reached 500 before the first of the golf courses opened in January 1986.

As Ernie Vossler recalls, "The development climate was right when we launched PGA WEST. La Quinta was a newly incorporated city. The City of La Quinta, County of Riverside and Coachella Valley Water District provided the governmental cooperation to make needed improvements to the site. In turn, we brought the new city an infusion of high-end housing and the allure of PGA-caliber golf excitement. It was truly a perfect match, and still is."

Since then, PGA WEST has played host to the Bob Hope Chrysler Classic, The Skins Game, Liberty Mutual Legends of Golf, Diners Club Matches, and the PGA Club Professional Championship. In the 1999 Bob Hope Chrysler Classic, David Duval shot a PGA final-round record 59 on the Arnold Palmer Course to take the win.

Golf is not the only game in town. *Tennis Magazine* recently acclaimed PGA WEST's 20,000-square-foot health and racquet club with its 19 hard surface, clay and grass courts as one of the six best places in the country for tennis players to retire.

PGA WEST's Palmer Course at the
Bob Hope Chrysler Classic

Weiskopf Course Opens

Dedication of the Tom Weiskopf Course, from left, Jack Nicklaus, Arnold Palmer, Tom Weiskopf and Pete Dye.

Bob Hope Chrysler Classic

From left, Alice Cooper, John Daly, PGA Pro, Chris O'Donnal, Samuel L. Jackson, and the Hope Girls.

THE QUARRY

While PGA WEST was going high-profile to earn its title as the Western Home of Golf in America, avid golfer Bill Morrow was gathering investors to acquire 360 acres nearby for The Quarry, a very private golf club tucked into the Santa Rosa foothills. The site had been a working quarry used by Riverside County to extract rock for building roads.

During his extensive golfing travels, Bill Morrow met noted golf course designer Tom Fazio. Touring Fazio around the proposed Quarry site, Morrow asked Fazio if the property was worth pursuing. "Tom's reply was 'Not only is it worth it, this place is a

Simply Perfection

Perfect 10. I could really do something special with it.'"

"The Fazio-designed golf course celebrates the changes in topography that make our location unique," he continues. "The Quarry course is really three distinct playing areas that run from our original hold in the ground where the rock was mined to 400 feet above sea level."

During construction, contractors found

Art in Public Places

"The Don" by artist Bill Ware located on the corner of Washington and Avenue 48.

markings of the ancient Indian trail used by the Cahuilla to "commute" back and forth between the desert villages where they wintered and the summer encampments in the mountains where they took refuge from the heat.

Remains of a turn-of-the-century mine, complete with original equipment, were also discovered and incorporated into the landscape as a testament to the early western pioneers. Half a dozen bronze reproductions of Frederic Remington sculptures were dotted around the course, and the clubhouse was decorated with numerous desert artifacts.

Construction on the course started in June of 1993. Thanks to laying 4 million square feet of sod (at an additional $1 million) instead of waiting for grass to grow from seed, the course opened on New Year's Day 1994. The Quarry is the only golf course in the desert rated in *Golf Digest's* "Top 100 Courses" list.

RANCHO LA QUINTA

In 1994, the Drummond Company took over a project that was idled by financial problems. The proposed community was re-purposed into Rancho La Quinta, and went on to become a highly successful venture and host course for The Skins Game.

Grady Sparks, president of TD Desert Development. is bullish on La Quinta for both business and personal reasons. When he and his wife, Connie, came to the desert in 1993, they immediately fell in love with La Quinta's spectacular setting and serene atmosphere. From a developer's standpoint, the community also measured up nicely.

Rancho La Quinta Clubhouse

Says Sparks, "La Quinta officials had a clear understanding of people who want to create something special that embraces all things in life for all people. If I'm going to invest several million dollars in a new development, I have to ask myself where the best place is to do that. For me, the choice is easy. It's La Quinta."

When the last phase of Rancho La Quinta was wrapping up, Sparks approached City leaders about "expanding La Quinta's southern boundaries." The result of the conversation was an annexation that extended La Quinta's boundaries to the base of the mountains. Sparks is busy developing his second desert country club there - Andalusia at Coral Mountain.

Civic Pride

As the population of La Quinta grew, so did the need for a proper Civic Center. Seventeen acres of land was designated for a campus to include a new city hall, designed by Gruen Associates, a senior center and a public library, surrounding a public park. The park, with its lake, water feature and gazebo, was designed to serve as a venue for public events. It is the current home of the annual La Quinta Arts Festival, and lends itself nicely to offerings like the outdoor cinema, showing free movies on balmy desert nights.

The Civic Center dedication on November 13, 1993, drew a large crowd of residents. Mayor John Pena helped bury a time capsule containing such eclectic items as coupons and the TV listing magazine from *The Desert Sun*, a room key, margarita glass and maid's uniform from the La Quinta Resort, a TV cable box and remote control from Colony CableVision, a photo of the original city limits sign showing a population of 4,701, and the income statement from the La Quinta Rotary Club's March 1993 Chili Cook-off.

John Pena served as mayor for 16 years, starting in 1984, and remembers the City Hall dedication as one of the many accomplishments the young City achieved in a relatively short period of time. Says Pena, "When I assumed office, La Quinta had many challenges. There were unpaved roads, lack of infrastructure, no schools and only one major source of income from the La Quinta Hotel."

He continues, "We proceeded to develop a plan to make La Quinta a destination resort city focusing on quality development while preserving our environment — specifically the Santa Rosa Mountains. Our philosophy was to be a community-friendly

Busy corner of Washington Street and Highway 111, circa 1990s

city while maintaining the character of our rich past. The City Council along with many community leaders developed a strong foundation that has paid dividends for future residents."

SERVICES WITH A SMILE

The La Quinta Senior Center is an active meeting place and center for classes, seminars and special events throughout the year for adults 55 and over, as well as members of the general public. An on-going calendar of events offers everything from arts and crafts or computer classes to handy services like health screening clinics and legal advice.

Views of the Civic Center Campus

City of
La Quinta

GEM OF THE DESERT

City of La Quinta, Gem of the Desert.

ISBN-13: 978-0-9727572-3-2
ISBN-10: 0-9727572-3-6
90000
9 780972 757232

Art surrounds you in even some of the most unexpected places in La Quinta. Like a bridge you may be driving or riding over. The City of La Quinta commissioned Juan and Patrick Naverrette to design decorative bridge railings on Washington and Jefferson Streets. The design reflects the ruggedness of the Santa Rosa Mountains that surround La Quinta.

ISBN-13: 978-0-9727572-3-2
ISBN-10: 0-9727572-3-6
90000
9 780972 757232

SilverRock Resort is an Arnold Palmer Signature Course. Pictured is hole #10 from the tee looking out toward the fairway and green. Photo EatonKirk.com

ISBN-13: 978-0-9727572-3-2
ISBN-10: 0-9727572-3-6
90000
9 780972 757232

La Quinta is abundant with charming scenes to inspire stunning plein air art, which is art painted in the great outdoors. A view of the picturesque Civic Center Campus was captured on canvas by students of an art class at the La Quinta Senior Center.

ISBN-13: 978-0-9727572-3-2
ISBN-10: 0-9727572-3-6
90000
9 780972 757232

Since its opening in the summer of 2005, the La Quinta Public Library has issued an impressive 500 library cards per month, and circulated an average of 6,000 items each month. The collection of nearly 35,000 items includes books, magazines, reference materials, videos, DVDs, CDs and special interest publications.

Public safety is paramount to City leaders as well as citizens. The La Quinta Police Department continues to enhance its capabilities with community service officers for routine calls and non-emergencies, training for bicycle and motorcycle officers, and a dedicated Traffic Enforcement Team. COPs (Citizens On Patrol) volunteers assist with emergencies or disasters. The Fire Department shares state-of-the-art resources like an aerial ladder truck with neighboring cities to keep pace with the growing population.

While numerous City parks are available for organized sports, family picnicking, swimming and hiking, the Community Services Department recently conducted an extensive public workshop to determine the direction for future parks and open spaces. The La Quinta Park is the most heavily used park in the city with its lighted sports fields, playground, walking trail, skate park, basketball court, pavilion and "spray ground" water feature. Some 1,500 players regularly participate in soccer.

Coachella Valley Recreation and Parks District is joining forces with the Bureau of Reclamation to create the Coachella Valley's first archeological park at the base of Coral Mountain at Avenue 58 and Jefferson Street. Interpretive trails, picnic areas and a trailhead for serious hiking up Coral Mountain or the Boo Hoff Trail are part of the plan.

From the time of incorporation in 1982, La Quinta has committed itself to protecting the unspoiled backdrop of the majestic Santa Rosa Mountains. In 1989, the City Council passed the toughest hillside development ordinance in the valley. The law was backed up with a policy statement intended to preserve the pristine wilderness in perpetuity.

Public Library
20,000 square foot library opened in November, 2005.

Bruce Lee Memorial
Dedication, Courage, Honor, is the art piece by Roger Hopkins that was dedicated to fallen Deputy Bruce Lee in December 2005. Above, pictured left to right are Sgt. Randy Wevertz, Deputy Ishmael Celaya, and Deputy Jason McFadden.

Fire Department
City expands services to keep the community safe.

Gamby
Children pose with Gamby, the City's official mascot.

Expressions of Beauty

In 1990, the La Quinta City Council adopted an Art in Public Places ordinance, joining other communities in encouraging community beautification through fees levied on developers to fund large-scale art pieces in high-profile public places. This is art that is available to everyone in their daily life. You can find public art in front of country clubs, at shopping centers and in public parks.

Public art projects can include a wide array of media and materials including sculpture, mosaics, photographs, calligraphy, natural fiber, and much more. Standard fixtures such as gates, bridges, streetlights, and signage are often used as limited-edition artist pieces.

Edie Hylton is Community Services Director for the La Quinta Art In Public Places program. She sums up the program this way, "Founders intended for La Quinta to be a haven for artistic expression and appreciation for nature and the environment. Just as the annual La Quinta Arts Festival brings fine art into the public realm, our public art program instills beauty around us every day."

Nature as art is represented by the Fred Wolff Bear Creek Nature Preserve, a 19-acre open area at the top of the cove set aside for dog walking, hiking and outdoor enjoyment. A flat, paved urban trail winds around the base of the mountains, providing

Art in Public Places
Bronze sculpture "Cahuilla Family" by Felicia.

Art in Public Places
Bronze sculpture "Spirit of La Quinta" by John Kennedy.

Art in Public Places
Art piece by Bill Ware honors veterans, sport figures and artists.

Art in Public Places
Spray Towers "Between Earth and Sky, Water Gives Life to All Creators," by Alber De Matteis and Kim Emerson.

an ideal place to exercise your pooch or simply enjoy some quiet time just steps from civilization.

The preserve was named after Fred Wolff, La Quinta's first mayor, in 2006. Wolff's love for the La Quinta cove began in 1949, when his parents built a vacation home that became his permanent residence until his death in 2004. His wife, Kay, still lives there and walks the Bear Creek trail regularly.

WORDS AND MUSIC

In the late 1980s, Fred Rice used his Hollywood music industry contacts to publish an album called "I Hear La Quinta Calling Me," featuring 10 versions of the title song, performed in styles ranging from pop to bassa nova. The country track was sung by Trisha Yearwood.

The words by Stephen Michael Portugal said in part, "The desert breezes sing of love. And silver stars shine high above - La Quinta. The swaying palms remind me too.

Lee Trevino's Hole-In-One
Hole #17, Alcatraz, at PGA WEST, TPC Stadium Golf Course.

Of what it means to say "I love you" - in La Quinta. I hear La Quinta calling me."

Since every great lyric deserves an equally great parody, the opportunity came on the final day of the 1987 Skins Game at PGA WEST. Lee Trevino made a hole-in-one on the 17th hole to pick up a $175,000 skin and end the day winning $310,000.

Comedy writer Gene Moss penned the parody lyrics which said in part, "I always will remember, that beautiful November in La Quinta. The day was bright and sunny,

when they handed me the money, in La Quinta. The course designed by Peter Dye, it nearly used to make me cry, until that day. Now PGA WEST is the place I love best. I hear La Quinta calling Lee, to play in Skins Game number three. Last year it was so good for me, I hear La Quinta calling Lee."

THE PLAY'S THE THING

In 1996, Honey Atkins served as a member of the La Quinta Cultural Commission. The idea of a community-based performing arts coalition was encouraged by the City Council. Honey and her husband, Rob, worked with others to form an active theatre group. The result was La Quinta On Stage.

La Quinta Historical Society Gala
From left, Fred Rice, Honey Atkins, Dottie Rice and Rob Atkins, circa 2000.

Their efforts really took shape as the La Quinta PlayHouse in 2004 when JoAnn Reeves brought her artistic directing experience to the group to stage a play depicting the in-studio radio version of "A Christmas Carol," at the La Quinta Hotel. With overwhelming patron support, the group held a 5-play season in a tent on the lawn at Old Town, ending in March of 2006.

The La Quinta PlayHouse reaches well beyond community theatre to provide on-going summer education programs for children from 8 to 17. Workshops include voice, movement and choreography. The future looks even brighter as plans are coming together for a black box theatre at SilverRock Resort. The public performance space will encompass 7,000 square feet and can be configured for a variety of uses.

PlayHouse
Noemi Hane, the La Quinta PlayHouse children's director, with, from left, Christian, Miranda and Victoria Hane.

A Place to Call Home

La Quinta is one of the Coachella Valley's youngest and fastest growing cities. It started with just over 5,000 residents in 1982, and showed a permanent population of nearly 40,000 in 2006. La Quinta showed the largest percentage increase in population - 52% - in the entire region since the 2000 Census.

Census figures report that 64% of the city's population is under 44 years old. Nevertheless, trends show the city's median age increasing as more baby boomers retire to the desert resort communities. Says City Manager Tom Genovese, "Making La Quinta a special place for residents of all ages and backgrounds is important to all of us. We strive to provide an unparalleled quality of life."

Affordable housing is one component of the City's plan. Just over 1,000 units of affordable housing for people with low or moderate incomes are now available or on the drawing board. Some are apartments with rental assistance, others are dedicated housing developments geared toward seniors or families. An additional 800 units are being planned for in the next 5 to 10 years. Great care is being given to insure that the housing projects fit well with the neighborhoods they will serve.

The City has three successful projects underway. Watercolors, a single family home complex for those 55 years and older, was recently completed and has received wide acclaim. The Vista Dunes Courtyard Homes development creates a convenient and affordable neighborhood within walking distance of La Quinta High School. The Coachella Valley Housing Coalition teamed up with the City to develop a 218 unit multi-family apartment community that provides convenient access to shopping and services.

La Quinta, One of the Fastest Growing Cities

Vista Dunes Mobile Park

Opened as a private travel trailer park, Vista Dunes has been reclaimed for housing to serve very low income families. Photo circa 1958.

Movin' on Up

 A number of upscale housing developments and country clubs are coming on line or expanding as La Quinta continues to be a desirable destination. Build-out continues at Trilogy, Mountain View, Tradition, PGA WEST, as well as smaller properties throughout the city. The Casitas Las Rosas vacation villas at Embassy Suites near Old Town offer yet another ownership alternative.

New residential communities are breaking ground, not only with the advent of new construction, but in style and appeal as well. Andalusia at Coral Mountain, a 1,000-acre luxury golf community, captures the distinctive heritage, colors and textures of the Andalusia region in Spain. The Madison Club at Avenue 54 and Madison Street promises to embody the highest levels of service and privacy required by the select clientele who choose it as their home.

Entertainment mogul Merv Griffin is taking a different approach with his Griffin Ranch, also at Avenue 54 and Madison Street. Instead of vast green fairways, Griffin is calling upon his love of thoroughbred horses to create a high-end home community focused around pastureland and riding facilities.

Equestrian enthusiasts will be drawn to Griffin Ranch with its Saddle Club facility boasting two arenas, dressage areas, and enough air-conditioned boarding space for 78 horses. Plans call for 300 homes ranging from 3,000 to nearly 6,000 square feet to be built by Trans West Housing, plus 20 one-acre custom "ranchettes" surrounding Griffin's private 40-acre estate.

Andalusia at Coral Mountain
Racquet Club & Fitness Center.

Trilogy at La Quinta

Griffin Ranch - Trans West

Good for Growth

While residents understandably look to their City government to provide code enforcement, public safety, and street repairs, it is economic development that pays the bills for those and other public services. 2007 marks the 12th year of the City of La Quinta's current economic development initiatives, designed to attract businesses which pay fees and taxes into the General Fund.

City Manager Tom Genovese explains it this way. "The City, acting through its Redevelopment Agency, negotiates with builders and developers to protect the City's interests and gain maximum return on its investment. This generates General Fund revenues, which fund programs like parks and recreation, street improvements, public safety, and other lifestyle amenities important to residents."

"Economic development," Genovese continues, "is a long-term strategy. Some projects take years to bring to fruition due to market forces, the financial climate and even forces of nature. Our goal is to continue to balance high-quality, revenue-generating development with the preservation of La Quinta's quality of life."

La Quinta's Community Development Director Doug Evans plays an instrumental role in implementing the City's short- and long-range economic development strategies. To do so, he is addressing the plan as four separate "villages" - the La Quinta Resort with its lodging, residential villas, shopping and dining;

Old Town in the village, a shopping and dining destination surrounded by residential and light commercial activity; SilverRock Resort, a golf and resort destination with nearby residential development; and the unincorporated areas within La Quinta's sphere of influence that could one day be stand-alone destinations of their own.

Looking ahead to the potential of traffic congestion, the City introduced a Golf Cart Transportation Plan as part of its 2003 General Plan update. The plan would provide marked paths along existing streets and charging stations at various commercial locations to allow residents to use their golf carts instead of automobiles. Future routes could encompass multi-use bike and equestrian paths and trails to provide even greater reach.

DESERT SANDS UNIFIED SCHOOL DISTRICT SERVES LA QUINTA

High Schools: Horizon High on Dune Palms Road and La Quinta High on Westward Ho Drive

Middle Schools: Colonel Mitchell Paige Middle on Palm Royale Drive, Horizon Middle on Dune Palms Road and La Quinta Middle on Avenue 50

Elementary Schools: John Adams Elementary on Desert Club Drive, Benjamin Franklin Elementary on Calle Tampico, Horizon Elementary on Dune Palms Road and Harry S. Truman Elementary on Avenue 50

LA QUINTA AT A GLANCE

Population: as of January 1, 2006 - 38,340
Population projections: 2010 44,700, 2015 50,200, 2020 54,500, 2025 59,400
Median age: Current - 36, 1990 - 32.2, 1980 - 27.1
Median household income: (2005) - $65,844
Retail Sales: in 2005 - $603.1 million
Assessed valuation: (FY 2005-06) - $7.81 billion
Total hotel room sales: (2005) - $41.236 million
• La Quinta has the highest daily ($122.40) and annual ($44,676) per room revenue in the Coachella Valley.
• La Quinta is home to the largest hotel in the Coachella Valley - the La Quinta Resort & Club
2006 traffic counts: (2-way, average daily trips)
Washington Street @ Highway 111 - 45,981
Washington Street @ Fred Waring Drive - 50,837
Highway 111 @ Adams Street - 41,302
Jefferson Street @ Avenue 48 - 28,045
Surrounding Population (April 2005)
Within 5 miles - 139,452, 10 miles, 15 miles - 302,885

SOURCES: CITY OF LA QUINTA AND WHEELER'S

LA QUINTA GOLF COURSES

Citrus
Dunes*
Indian Springs*
La Quinta Country Club
Madison Club
Mountain*
Mountain View Country Club
Nicklaus Course at PGA WEST (2)
Norman Course at PGA WEST*
Palmer Course at PGA WEST
Palm Royale*
Jones Course at Rancho La Quinta
Pete Course at Rancho La Quinta
SilverRock Resort*
Stadium Course at PGA WEST*
The Hideaway (2)
The Palms
The Quarry
Tradition
Trilogy at La Quinta*
Weiskopf Course at PGA WEST
Open to the public

Spotlight on SilverRock Resort

As golf communities throughout the Coachella Valley proliferated, La Quinta civic leaders recognized the opportunity to create a public golf venue that would also provide the City with an economic stimulus. In the mid-1990s, market studies were conducted to determine whether or not La Quinta could support a public golf, hotel and retail development.

Not only did the studies confirm the viability of such a project, they indicated that potential revenue from such a venture would be essential to meeting future needs of such a rapidly growing community. In 1996, resort/recreation development was included in the City's economic development plan.

In 2002, redevelopment funds were used to purchase 525 acres from KSL Resorts, obtain environmental permits and create a master plan for future development. The Arnold Palmer Classic Course at SilverRock Resort broke ground in 2004, and was named by *Golf Magazine* in 2005 as one of the "Top 10 New Courses That You Can Play." It was the only golf course in California to make the list.

A legion of "Arnie's Army" golf fans came out for the grand opening of the Arnold Palmer Classic Course at SilverRock Resort on March 1, 2005. The City Council began working exclusively with Lowe Destination Development to bring a four-star boutique hotel, four-star luxury hotel, private casitas, and retail village to the site. Lowe, through its dedicated LDD SilverRock LLC, is expected to invest more than $500 million in the master-planned resort.

PHOTOGRAPHER MARC GLASSMAN

SilverRock Resort Ground Breaking

From left, Council Member Lee Osborne, Mayor Don Adolph, Arnold Palmer, Council Member Terry Henderson, Council Member Stanley Sniff and Assemblyman John Benoit.

Landmark Golf Company

From left, SilverRock Resort's management company, Joe Walser, Jr., Ernie Vossler, Judy Vossler, Arnold Palmer, Andy Vossler and Johnny Pott.

Opening Day

The hotels and retail development will take several years to complete on 60 of SilverRock Resort's 525 acres. In all, the site will boast 600 rooms and more than 80,000 square feet of retail space. The City estimates it will receive a return on its investment of $50 million in bed and sales tax and $34 million in tax increment revenues over the first 10 years.

PHOTOGRAPHER JOHN KIRKPATRICK

SilverRock Resort, Arnold Palmer Classic Course, Hole #10

Places to Stay and Play

Old Town La Quinta harkens back to a simpler time when people lived, worked and shopped without getting in their cars. More specifically, Old Town La Quinta is a faithful re-creation of what the village of La Quinta was designed to become in the 1930s. Its Spanish architecture and quaint design are patterned after the La Quinta Resort - the destination that gave La Quinta its name and first identity.

Developer Wells Marvin sees his Old Town shopping destination as a people connection. "It's much more humanizing if you can work in a village than an office park," he observes. His "new urbanism" homage to the past has been widely praised at organizations like the Urban Land Institute and the National Association of Home Builders.

Phase Two of Old Town doubles the retail and office space, adding a broader complement of merchandise and services by day and dining and entertainment options by night.

The La Quinta name is synonymous with hospitality. After all, the city was named after the elegant La Quinta Hotel. And, for years, the hotel was the only game in town. The venerable resort has now been joined by two other hotels with more accommodations on the near horizon.

A 14.5 acre Embassy Suites property with 146 hotel suites and a 5,000-square-foot spa is open for business near the Old Town shopping district.

Homewood Suites by Hilton La Quinta on Washington Street and Miles Avenue features 130 suites geared toward the extended stay guest, with daily hot breakfast, 24-hour business center and convenience shop, and on-site laundry.

Plans were recently approved for 61 acres at SilverRock Resort for a condo-hotel, resort hotel, retail village and black-box performing arts theater. The condo-hotel is expected to break ground in 2008.

La Quinta Resort & Club

Homewood Suites by Hilton La Quinta

Old Town La Quinta

Partners in Progress

Retail follows rooftops. That's the common philosophy of commercial land development. Likewise, health and human service providers set up shop where there's a critical mass of consumers.

In the early 1990s, Auto Club of Southern California (AAA) president Tom McKernan was a part-time La Quinta resident, and Richard Jandt was the local Auto Club manager. Jandt remembers Mr. McKernan hand-picking the site at the corner of Washington Street and Highway 111 for a new office. Says Jandt, "After the La Quinta office opened in July of 1993, we went from serving 125 visitors each day to 425 by 2001. Our location became the flagship of the 90 Auto Club offices in Southern California."

When Wal-Mart was looking for a location to introduce their superstore concept into California in the early 2000s, they chose La Quinta for the expansion into the state.

Costco Wholesale's 500th location opened for business at 8 a.m. on November 22, 2006, at the corner of Highway 111 and Jefferson Street. Warehouse manager Bill Silvester celebrated the occasion by saying, "The La Quinta city motto, 'Gem of the Desert,' could not be more appropriate for the opening of our 500th location."

Eisenhower Medical Center is developing 14 acres of land on Washington Street and Miles Avenue into a community health facility next to the Homewood Suites hotel. The ambulatory care center will not include beds for overnight hospital stays, but it will encompass 300,000 square feet of medical services.

An urgent care center will utilize the latest screening and diagnostic technologies. An outpatient surgery center, imaging and diagnostic testing facilities, physician offices, and ancillary support services will be on site. Says Michael Landes, president of the Eisenhower Medical Center Foundation, "Our physicians want to practice in La Quinta. There is a need to recruit new physicians for new patients. This facility will give us the ability to do that. We're looking for a balance of physicians to serve the community."

Eisenhower Medical Center
Rendering of facility to open in 2008 on Washington.

In the Marketplace
Total retail sales are projected to reach $620 million per year before 2010.

Enduring Images

Frank Capra loved La Quinta, and he expressed his love for his adopted desert home this way in his autobiography, *The Name Above The Title:*

"I walked and walked over the purple sand dunes. Spring had come to the desert. To honor its coming, the dunes unrolled verbena carpets of royal purple. Ocotillos raised their thorny spears tipped with heads of hallelujah scarlet. I walked and walked. Startled jackrabbits leaped twice, then stood upright, eyeing me curiously. Those clowning birds, the roadrunners, peeked around the sage inviting me to play hide and seek. I walked and walked over the purple sand dunes."

In 1997, the La Quinta Historical Society asked high school students to submit poems reflecting the theme "How I Can Be Part of the La Quinta Story." The winning entry came from Marissa Krause for her poem, "I Am La Quinta."

"I AM LA QUINTA"

I am the past, present and future of La Quinta - reflected in each sunrise and sunset, the cactus blooms of springs and the clear, starry night skies.

I have lived here my entire life and wish to preserve the desert way. I have grown, nurtured and been protected by our majestic Santa Rosas.

I open my heart and listen to the ancient wisdom of Cahuilla grandmothers and the pleading howls of brother coyote.

I am part of La Quinta, just like you. Be proud, be strong and help keep the magic alive in beauty…La Quinta.

- Marissa Krause

OFFICIAL BIRD, TREE AND FLOWER

Gambel's Quail

Quail can go without drinking water by feeding on small fruits, green buds, and insects. Gambel's quail was named for William Gambel, a 19th century naturalist who first recorded the species' identification. The birds can be found as far east as Colorado and as far south as Mexico.

Smoke Tree

The smoke tree can grow to 20 feet tall with an intricate mass of spiny gray-green branches that look like puffs of smoke from a distance. In summer, the trees flower with bright blue-purple blooms. A member of the pea family, the smoke tree flowers during summer with bright blue-purple blooms.

Sand Verbena

The plants bloom from February to May, especially after abundant winter rains, with a bright pink, trumpet-shaped flower. The stalks of the plant are sticky and have hairy "creepers" that allow them to expand outward along the ground. Verbena can carpet open desert washes for miles after a good soaking.

The Best Is Yet to Come

In January of 2007, the City Council signed off on a $550 million multi-phase agreement that had been in the works since 2005 with Lowe Destination Development for a hotel resort project at SilverRock. It will include a 230-unit boutique condo-hotel, spa and executive conference facility; a four- or five-story resort hotel with 90 luxury rooms and 180 condo-hotel units; and a retail village with 40,000 square feet of retail space, 12,000 square feet of restaurant space, and 28,000 square feet appropriate for office space or various flexible uses.

SilverRock Dream Team

From left, Council Member Tom Kirk, Chairman of Redevelopment Agency and Council Member Lee Osborne, Council Member Terry Henderson, President of Lowe Destination Development Desert Inc. Ted Lennon, Mayor Don Adolph, Chief Operations Officer of Lowe Destination Development Desert Inc. Tom Cullinan, Vice President and Development Manager of SilverRock Resort/Lowe Destination Development Desert Inc. Tom Devlin.

La Quinta City Council 2007

From left, Council Member Lee Osborne, Mayor Pro Tem Stanley Sniff, Council Member Terry Henderson, Council Member Tom Kirk and Mayor Don Adolph.

> *SilverRock Resort will rise on "the finest piece of property" in the Coachella Valley.*
> —TED LENNON, PRESIDENT, LOWE DESTINATION DEVELOPMENT

> *"We're all on the same page, moving in the same direction."*
> —COUNCIL MEMBER TERRY HENDERSON

> *"It'll be outstanding, a first-class development."*
> —MAYOR DON ADOLPH

LA QUINTA MAYORS

1982 - 2007

Fred Wolff, May 1, 1982
Bob Baier, April 5, 1983
Larry Allen, April 3, 1984
Judith Cox, November 22, 1984
John Pena, November 19, 1985

William Hoyle, November 18, 1986
John Pena, November 29, 1988
Glenda Bangerter Holt, Dec. 4, 1995
John Pena, November 24, 1997
John Pena, December 5, 2000
Don Adolph, December 3, 2002
Don Adolph, December 7, 2004
Don Adolph, December 5, 2006

Archeologists discovered a spot at the base of the mountains near the cove they believe was used by native Cahuilla women as a gathering place to grind corn and talk about the news of the day. The location has been dubbed Talking Rock.

Even until today, the people of La Quinta gather to talk - in restaurants, school yards, groceries stores, places of worship, and at City Hall. On behalf of the La Quinta City Council, we thank you for 25 wonderful years of community spirit. The best is yet to come.

CHAPTER FIVE

With a backdrop by Mother Nature, art, culture and commerce come together in La Quinta.

Those Who Make A Difference

La Quinta is widely known as a vibrant community set in a place of natural beauty that inspires creativity and prosperity for residents and visitors alike. From its history of hospitality and world-class recreation to its new-found success as a retail and professional hub, La Quinta continues to shine.

The La Quinta Chamber of Commerce puts it this way. "A progressive group of residents and business people are dedicated to our city's success. You'll find compelling reasons to stay - strong business and residential growth, civic well-being and a fantastic quality of life."

Andalusia at Coral Mountain

Since 1993, Grady Sparks and his development team have literally been shaping the future of La Quinta in both dramatic and significant ways. Early that year, TD Desert Development, an affiliate of Drummond Real Estate, purchased 700 acres of land bordered by 48th Avenue, 50th Avenue, Washington Street and Jefferson Street. They began immediately to turn this property into one of the most successful luxury golf communities ever created in the Coachella Valley, Rancho La Quinta.

Today, Rancho La Quinta is an established, upscale private community, offering a wide range of custom-quality homes, a world-class Racquet Club & Fitness Center, two championship golf courses, one by Robert Trent Jones, Jr. and the other by US Open champion Jerry Pate, and a private 20,000 sq.ft. Clubhouse complex for club members and their guests.

In 2003, with Rancho La Quinta nearing a sell-out of its approximately 900 homes, TD Desert Development began assembling another 1,000 acres of prime land in South La Quinta, land that is surrounded on three sides by the spectacular Santa Rosa Mountains, and bordered by Madison Street, Avenue 58, Avenue 60 and Monroe Street. This new community development, to be called "Andalusia at Coral Mountain," would be inspired in its design by the architectural details and lifestyle of Andalusia, a historic region adjacent to the Mediterranean in southern Spain.

Determined to "get it right," Mr. Sparks led several key members of his design and marketing team on a five-day tour of the Andalusia region. "We had a Spanish architect who served as a guide to take us to key places in southern Spain – including Seville, Marbella, Ronda and Mijas, "explained Sparks." The team met on a daily basis after each tour to discuss what design elements we wanted to use in our new community."

These special Andalusian details include custom hand-painted tiles, wrought iron doors and hand-made entry gates, elegant entry courtyards, sculpted soffits, built-in niches and arched passageways between rooms to name just a few.

Connie & Grady Sparks

"We are making Andalusia at Coral Mountain something truly special."

Other Andalusian details include use of the popular olive trees of Spain as a featured element on the golf courses. Paella and other tasty tapas will appear on the clubhouse menu. Street names and model home names have also been taken from the towns and villages in this popular province of Spain.

"This property was flat as a table when we bought it," commented TD Desert Development President Grady Sparks. "To make this something really special, we had to go the extra step, to give it character. To date, more than seven million cubic yards of dirt have been moved in the making of the community and the first golf course. Hundreds of olive trees and date palms were installed. Tens of thousands of fragrant flowers and other plants grace the topography,

and a magnificent waterfall makes a memorable finish at the 18th green."

"Now, when you go out to the seventh tee you'll see the dramatic undulations and different elevations of the homes. To stand up there now and see this spectacular landscape is very satisfying. We are making Andalusia at Coral Mountain something truly special."

When Andalusia at Coral Mountain opened for sale in the Spring of 2006, the community presented six luxurious model homes, the first of two private golf courses by internationally renowned architect Rees Jones, several miles of hiking and biking trails throughout the 1,000 acres of the community, and a Racquet Club & Fitness Center under construction that will offer 19,000 square feet of indoor and outdoor recreational and entertainment areas.

Built around a series of courtyards, the Center will highlight many gathering places to enjoy our relaxing desert lifestyle. Situated adjacent to the first golf course and currently scheduled for completion in late Spring 2007,

the Center will offer its resident members and their guests a long list of amenities, including indoor and outdoor dining rooms, a lounge, Pro Shops for both tennis and golf, a Fitness Center with state-of-the-art equipment, nine tennis courts (clay and HarTru surfaces), a 25-meter swimming pool, two separate wading pools, a therapy spa, sunbathing gazebos, and relaxing cabanas.

Several members of the management team have purchased homes within Andalusia at Coral Mountain, including President Grady Sparks and his wife, Connie. Both are natives of Alabama but have lived in La Quinta since 1993, and consider themselves to be year-around residents at Andalusia. They are supporters of the Children's Hunger Fund, Jordan Outreach Ministries, and are members of Southwest Community Church.

In addition to Rancho La Quinta, the company has also created successful, award-winning golf communities in Vestavia Hills, Alabama, and Lakeland, Florida. Andalusia is the latest community by TD Desert Development, L.P., an affiliate of Drummond Company, one of America's largest privately held natural resource companies and listed by Forbes Magazine as one of the top 500 privately owned companies in the United States. Andalusia promises to be the crown jewel in the developer's crown.

Arnold Palmer's

With all the world-class golf courses in La Quinta, it just seemed fitting that Arnold Palmer would choose the area as the location for his superb restaurant.

Since 2003, Arnie's army of fans have been celebrating his career milestones and enjoying elegant comfort cuisine at Arnold Palmer's.

Open daily for dinner, the legend's restaurant boasts five dining rooms done in traditional club décor with names such as The British Open, The Masters and The U.S. Open. Photographs and memorabilia from these major golf tournaments are showcased in each room. Cozy fireplaces, rich wood floors and a colorful courtyard add to the ambiance. Arnie's Pub, with its own Pub Menu, is a popular meeting spot with nightly entertainment by Kevin Henry.

A big attraction is a nine hole putting green that is adjacent to a large outdoor patio. Both are blessed with stunning views of the Santa Rosa Mountains.

Executive Chef and General Manager Brett Maddock was the first one hired. He,

along with Restaurant Manager Dodi Henry and Managing Partner David Chapman, worked with Palmer in establishing the restaurant's vision.

Maddock's passion for cooking began when he worked for a butcher shop in Lake Elmo, Minn. Soon he was enrolled in the Culinary Arts Program at St. Paul College. After working in several well-known restaurants throughout the Minneapolis area, he joined The Ritz-Carlton and honed is culinary skills at The Terrace Restaurant in Naples, Fla., and The Dining Room in Buckhead, Ga. He came to the Palm Springs area and wowed locals and guests with his sumptuous light cuisine at The Lodge in Rancho Mirage.

"At Arnold Palmer's our menu is actually three menus in one," Maddock says. "It consists of Steak House Selections, Chef's Features and Arnie's Favorites."

Pan Seared Sea Scallops and Braised Beef Short Ribs are signature dishes of the executive chef while Arnie's Favorites include Traditional Meatloaf with Mashed Potatoes, Broccoli and Gravy.

"Arnie is very much involved," Maddock says. "He loves to eat and he appreciates simple comfort food."

In fact, the restaurant's extensive wine list, which has received the coveted Wine Spectator Award of Excellence, has Arnold Palmer private label Chardonnay, Cabernet Sauvignon and Reserve Cabernet vintages.

With the variety of venues, banquets for 20 or more are held frequently. Local in-home catering is also available.

"I spend a lot of time in the dining room getting to know a lot of people. It's fun for me, and there are always good vibes to be shared," Maddock adds.

California Lifestyle Realty

Ask Gene Darr, vice president of brokerage at California Lifestyle Realty, what he and his more than 30 realtors are selling and he will without hesitation say "lifestyle."

With prime locations at the legendary La Quinta Resort & Club, in Old Town and at the PGA WEST Stadium and Mountain/Dunes clubhouses, California Lifestyle Realty focuses on resort properties and custom homes, along with short and long-term leases, in the La Quinta Club communities and PGA WEST.

Unlike traditional real estate offices, these are more like user-friendly galleries. They are gathering places where guests of the resort and visitors to the restaurants and shops within the resort and community are welcome to come in and ask questions about La Quinta, inquire about club memberships, take a tour or just pick up literature on available properties throughout the Coachella Valley.

"Most of our realtors live in La Quinta and are enthusiastic about introducing prospects to all the good things it has to offer. Nothing is high pressure. It is a very casual, low-key environment. We are here to expand on the visitor's experience," Darr says.

Owned by CNL Hospitality Properties, Inc., an Orlando-based real estate investment trust, the lifestyle galleries have their own identities. The 1,200-square-foot

headquarters at La Quinta Resort & Club boasts a huge topography model that provides an overview of nearby golf courses and luxury resort communities including The Citrus, Santa Rosa Cove and PGA WEST.

"Many of the resort guests who stop in aren't even thinking about purchasing a home. They say they are 'just looking, not buying.' Often they're repeat guests who are well aware of the wonderful weather, world-class golf and close proximity to Los Angeles and Las Vegas. Before you know it they have purchased a second or third home. The timing was right for them."

As for the Old Town gallery, it is more high-tech with multiple-screen projections of lifestyle pictures and homes for sale and lease that anyone strolling by in the evening can view.

The golf clubhouse locations are perfect for guests who have finished a round of golf, are fascinated by the lifestyle and want to learn more. There is on-going interaction between the realtors and membership sales professionals, for a membership purchase might precede a home buy or vice versa.

"When it comes to La Quinta lifestyle, we know the territory better than anyone," Darr says.

The Citrus Club at La Quinta Resort™

Picture groves of fragrant grapefruit, orange and lemon trees skirted with white trunks. Add a charming Spanish-style clubhouse, lush green fairways and a stunning background of majestic mountains and you have The Citrus Club, a private club defined by world-class golf, warm friendships and a special connection to the legendary La Quinta Resort & Club.

Its centerpiece is the Pete Dye-designed Citrus Course complete with numerous water hazards, rolling terrain and sand bunkers that combine to make 7,000 yards of challenge, intrigue and memories.

The clubhouse is a delightful blend of quaint and contemporary with splendid archways, brilliant bougainvillea and soothing fountains. Its design is in keeping with the club's historic sister property, La Quinta Resort & Club. On the drawing board are plans for a 2,600-square-foot fitness center that will sport its own group exercise room. Four tennis courts will also be added along with a feature bar with its own firepit and extended outdoor seating that will allow for panoramic views of this storybook setting.

Member amenities are rich and many, including preferred pricing on room accommodations at the resort as well as at resort pro shops and restaurants. Privileges extend to the use of the resort's spectacular tennis and fitness facilities and to Spa La Quinta with its relaxing wellness treatments many of which are citrus-scented.

Memberships are also varied. Citrus and Heritage Golf Memberships allow for unlimited golf on the Citrus, Mountain and Dunes courses where there is a cap of 350 per private course. La Quinta Resort's Mountain Course, literally carved out of a mountain, is renowned for its challenge and beauty, while the resort's scenic Dunes is a links-style course that rests at the foot of the Santa Rosas. In addition to play on these three Pete Dye courses, Desert Membership privileges include unlimited play on all courses at The Club at PGA WEST. There is also a Junior Golf Membership for those under age 45.

Social members participate in a myriad of activities that include holiday parties, cooking classes and jazz concerts. They enjoy unlimited access to the resort's fitness center, pools, spa facilities and tennis along with access at preferred rates to the Mountain, Dunes, Nicklaus, Stadium and Norman courses.

The Citrus Club is an enchanting place to connect with friends and be part of La Quinta's history.

PHOTOGRAPHER MARK PALMER

Custom Vintage Wine Cellars Inc.

Throughout her 25 years in the Coachella Valley, Gina McGuire has been part of the area's phenomenal growth. Her interior design firm, McGuire and Associates, has worked closely with TD Desert Development and Drummond Company to create elegant interiors for model homes and special projects in The Estancias at Rancho La Quinta and Andalusia at Coral Mountain. For Andalusia, the McGuire design team also was involved in the interior design of its racquet club and clubhouse.

McGuire noted that her clients liked to entertain at home and wine collecting appeared to be a growing trend. Clients increasingly were requesting, not just racking, but custom-designed wine cellars that would satisfy their individual needs.

So, McGuire shifted her focus and created Custom Vintage Wine Cellars. Interior design is still part of her business but it is now limited to models, spec homes and clubhouses.

"I find that people wanting a custom wine cellar usually already have a room designated to be a wine room be it a den, pantry or just any room they aren't using," McGuire says. "Today many architects and builders incorporate a wine room into their floor plans."

The value is in the unique product and the one-stop shopping experience Custom Vintage Wine Cellars has to offer. They provide a myriad of mechanics including vapor barrier, cooling systems, thermostats, electrical-all the necessities to create a room that is temperature and humidity regulated.

"Custom" is key for there are many different ways to personalize a collection. Bottles can be showcased in diamond bins, case box or vertical storage, sloped reveal displays or with special cabinetry for treasured single bottles. Racking is available in a variety of woods from the popular all-heart redwood to exotic woods like purple heart, jarrah or black walnut.

McGuire's interior design skills are utilized in the aesthetics of the room. There are a variety of wall veneers, flooring and ceiling details as well as decorative features such as wood or iron doors. Custom hardware, furniture and accessories must also be considered.

In addition to walk-in cellars, Custom Vintage Wine Cellars also designs free-standing or built-in storage cabinets in a variety of styles.

Prospective clients can get a sampling of various options and styles in the store's 5,000-square-foot showroom in Palm Desert.

"We're all about creating a special room that is aesthetically pleasing and fulfills one's storage needs. We have a great team of craftsmen whom we have worked with for years. Together we can get pretty spectacular."

Desert House Call Physicians

It seems fitting that Dr. Peter M. Kadile, who considers himself an "old-fashioned" type family physician, would locate his private family medical practice in Old Town La Quinta. "The concept of Old Town appealed to me and fits in with what I offer," Dr. Kadile says.

What Dr. Kadile, a board certified family physician, offers is a refreshing, more personal approach to quality primary care that takes into account the busy lifestyles of both residents and visitors. In addition to seeing patients in his La Quinta office, Dr. Kadile makes house calls in the privacy and comfort of homes, offices and visitors' hotel rooms.

He has seen firsthand overcrowded emergency rooms, busy Urgent Cares and overwhelmed colleagues having to sandwich large numbers of patients into limited time frames, often resulting in long waits for patients.

His medical training began at Kirksville College of Osteopathic Medicine in Kirksville, Mo., where he attended under the Health Professions Scholarship Program with the U.S. Navy. After graduation he was commissioned a lieutenant and commenced an internship in General Surgery at Naval Medical Center Oak Knoll and University of California-Davis East Bay Program in Oakland, Calif. Upon completion he underwent U.S. Naval Flight Surgeon training at Pensacola, Fla., and was subsequently stationed with Marine Helicopter Training Squadron 303 in Camp Pendleton, Calif. When his tour was completed, he was accepted into the Family Practice residency program at

Naval Hospital Camp Pendleton. In 2000, he graduated with the rank of lieutenant commander and was stationed at Naval Hospital Twentynine Palms where he would become the department head for Primary Care and for the second time would be awarded the Navy Commendation Medal.

When Dr. Kadile left active duty, he joined the Kerrigan Family Medical Group in Palm Desert as a staff family physician and as medical director for Healthcare Express.

His Desert House Call Physicians, launched in 2006, functions as a fee for service medical practice specializing in doctor house calls, general primary care for patients of all ages and preventive medicine. Although health insurance is not accepted, patients can submit charges to their insurance company for partial reimbursement for the medical visit.

"This concept allows me to spend quality time with the patient. I am able to treat the 'whole person,' not just the symptoms. And it is convenient for the patient because there is no waiting. With the insurance equation out of the picture, it becomes all about good medicine."

Dolan Law Offices

John Patrick Dolan is a criminal trial lawyer with close to three decades of trial experience in the criminal courts of Los Angeles, Orange, San Bernardino and Riverside counties. He is also a California State Bar Certified Specialist in Criminal Law having passed an intensive series of tests, evaluations and requirements to qualify.

The author of 12 best-selling books, including the classic, *Negotiate like the Pros*™, Dolan is an internationally recognized expert on negotiation and conflict resolution and is a sought-after keynote speaker for business and legal professionals. In fact, he has been inducted by the National Speakers Association into the Professional Speakers Hall of Fame. A video sampling of his dynamic and often humorous presentation can be seen at www.negotiatelikethepros.com.

In addition, he is a popular legal news analyst and appears frequently on Fox News Channel, MSNBC and Court TV. John appears twice a week as the KMIR6 Legal News Analyst. On Saturday mornings his radio show, John Patrick Dolan's LawTalk L.A., is broadcast locally with plans for national syndication.

Irene, Dolan's wife of 35 years, is also busy managing LawTalk™ MCLE, a continuing legal education company that the couple founded in 1992. Their daughter, "A.J.," assists Dolan at his law office in Indio.

"I love the variety; however, the unifying factor in all that I do is my criminal law practice. Everything emanates from that," Dolan says.

After living in Orange County all of their lives, the Dolan family moved to La Quinta a few years ago and are delighted with the community.

"We are so centrally located and I'm able to do everything from this one location. It is a short trip to the local stations for my radio and TV broadcasts. With speaking engagements across the country, the convenience of the Palm Springs International Airport is terrific. And my wife has transformed our guest casita into headquarters for our continuing legal education company."

Dolan also appreciates the beauty and tranquility of La Quinta and the magnificent mountain views that greet him every day.

And, he has high praise for the pleasant collegial atmosphere he experiences at the Larson Justice Center in Indio.

After all these years practicing criminal law, his enthusiasm has never waned. "I love going to court. There is not a day that I don't think of how we make the Constitution come alive with this work. Being in court is the real thing."

Desert Life Styles Inc.

 A Renaissance man is defined as one with broad interests who is accomplished in many areas. This description aptly fits Kaveh Daryaie, whose diversity in design of custom home interiors, architecture, furniture and automobiles is boundless.

The culmination of his many careers, travels and hobbies is evidenced in his newest enterprise, Desert Life Styles, Designs by Kaveh. Kaveh's innovative facility, which accommodates Radio Active, an audio visual company, is a fully operating smart home. A smart home is one equipped with specially structured wiring that allows occupants to remotely control a myriad of automated home electronic devices by entering a single command.

"Everything works here. It's state of the art," Kaveh says.

In fact the showroom is truly a home with a fully equipped kitchen, one-of-a-kind bar, living and dining areas, powder room and artfully appointed theater. Each room is Internet ready. With the touch of a keypad, one can turn on lights, Jacuzzi, fireplace,

"Almost everything from fabrication of countertops, to the designing of furniture, upholstering, and the creation of fabrics is done at the facility by Kaveh and his team of professionals."

music and security, among other things. A remote device allows smart home owners to monitor and control their home environment while away.

This highly automated showroom concept was the brainchild of Kaveh and Mark Reulman, owner and president of Radio Active. "From texture to technology" is how Kaveh describes the successful meshing of disciplines.

Kaveh's interests have always had an artistic bent. Born in Iran, his parents emigrated to Pasadena in 1968 and his father, an upholsterer, laid the foundation for a successful business named Ray's Interiors & Home Furnishings. Kaveh, along with his brothers, would work at the store every day after school. His father was a strong proponent of "hands-on education."

Although Kaveh developed an early love of textiles, he yearned for a career in show business. At 17, while still working at the store, he began a career as a promoter and originated the idea of creating mobile DJ entertainment. Simultaneously he was honing his rolling skating skills at Venice Beach and was to become California state champion for three consecutive years. His group of skating professionals, The New Horizons, would go on to appear in movies such as Skatetown U.S.A., starring Scott Baio, and Xanadu with Olivia Newton-John. Eventually, they were purchased by Pepsi and their name was changed to the Aspen Disco Rollers. They went on tour and traveled to New Zealand, Australia and Venezuela. Kaveh also netted a $5,000 prize in a Dance Fever competition.

Still fascinated with design, Kaveh attended the Pasadena Art Institute and Pasadena City College. Always the entrepreneur, at one point he owned a limousine service.

By the early '90s, Kaveh was married and had a young family. He met his good friend and mentor Dave Roberts who owned Shutters & More in Rancho Mirage. Kaveh helped to grow the business and would later purchase it. Future ventures included La Mirage Interior Design in Rancho Mirage and Casa del Sol in Palm Desert.

Today Desert Life Styles is a summation of this Renaissance man. Here Kaveh makes dreams a reality introducing refined desert living to clients of international renown. Ever discriminating, Kaveh declines to name-drop, preferring to let his work speak for itself.

"I love what I do, but I need to know you before I'll work for you. I approach people with honesty. I help them discover what style or era they see

themselves living in. I want my clients to be pleased. At the end of the day they stay, I leave."

Almost everything from fabrication of countertops, to the designing of furniture, upholstering, and the creation of fabrics is done at the facility by Kaveh and his team of professionals.

Prior to the selection of design and materials, Kaveh has a three-step program that introduces his firm to prospective clients. Plan "A" consists of a two-hour home visit and evaluation. If it's a "go," the fee is applied toward the situation at hand. Plan "B" entails a three-hour home visit and two board-mounted renderings. If the decision is made to move forward, half of the fee goes into the project while the other half is retained for design purposes. In Plan "C" the client is provided with all the design concepts at which time this becomes part of the retainer system which works to keep both the designer and customer on the same page. A percentage of the total job becomes a retainer and as the retainer diminishes, it is replenished by the client until the job is complete.

Kaveh is also known for designing and customizing automobiles and motorcycles. He and his wife Lisa, who shares his love of bikes, are involved in many charitable fund-raising rides throughout Southern California.

"Along with my two kids, Blake and Paris, cars are my passion," says Kaveh, who has been known to own as many as a dozen cars and almost as many show bikes at one time.

Dyson & Dyson
Janine Stevens Realtor®

 Although born in Los Angeles, Janine Stevens considers herself a local homegrown product of the Coachella Valley. When she was eight, her family moved to the desert. Stevens attended primary, middle and high schools here as well as College of the Desert.

Stevens attributes much of her success as a top producer with Dyson & Dyson to her extensive knowledge of the Coachella Valley. Specifically, she has watched La Quinta grow from just a handful of country club communities to premier developments that include PGA WEST, Traditions and The Hideaway.

She is adamant about being personally involved with each and every transaction, whether large or small. She also believes that responsive follow-through has been paramount in achieving her goals. She goes the extra mile to make sure her clients are satisfied. She honed her communication skills plus determination to succeed early on in the '80s while still in high school when she worked her way up from box girl to checker at a local supermarket.

"I knew the grocery business wasn't in my future since I didn't want to be a store manager so I decided to step out in order to step forward," Stevens says.

After college, she opted for a retail position with La Quinta Hotel in its golf shop. During that time she acquired her real estate license in 1989 and she joined Landmark Real Estate and embarked on a career specializing in upscale country club communities in the La Quinta area.

"I learned a lot about golf while working at the golf shop. After all, I'm selling the entire golf lifestyle, not just homes. I'm selling communities in which golf plays a predominate role."

When Bob Dyson decided to open an office in La Quinta, Stevens was the first agent he recruited. That proved to be a smart move because in no time Stevens earned Top Sales Agent by Closed Volume and Top Earning

Agent by Gross Commissions Earned awards. In turn, Stevens gained access to the latest technology along with a unique agent and client support system that included agent services, marketing, escrow management and an in-house attorney.

Ever the champion in helping women succeed, she is active in Women Working Wonders, a local non-profit group organized to financially assist women in need in the Coachella Valley. She also belongs to Desert Estates Network, a local high-end luxury group of the top real estate agents in the Coachella Valley and Strathmore's Who's Who.

Ehline Development Co.

 The stunning beauty of the desert has always been a heartfelt attraction for Dick and Paul Ehline, brothers and principals of Ehline Development Company. Starting in the 1960s, the closely knit Ehline family found time to periodically escape the frenetic pace of their successful business to relax at their second home in the Coachella Valley.

Ehline Development Company, originally headquartered in Orange County, is considered one of the state's premier builders and developers with an impressive portfolio of commercial and residential properties throughout California.

Among these are the luxury communities of Somerset in Villa Park and Blackhawk in Danville as well as Plaza Lafayette, a prestigious lifestyle center in Tustin, which is the location for the popular Nieuport 17 restaurant.

"We have always prided ourselves in being cutting edge," Paul says.

"Great design is our passion and our homes be they custom or part of high-end residential communities are re-owned for their harmony with nature, as well as their elegance and fine craftsmanship."

Indeed, the Ehline difference has been in the superior attention to detail when it comes to design, building, construction and service.

It was good planning and land for sale in La Quinta that precipitated a shift in the company's future. Paul spotted several outstanding properties and made the purchase. The company relocated its headquarters to La Quinta.

Why La Quinta? "We think La Quinta is the future," Dick says. "It has a stellar reputation and truly is the gem of the desert."

In a short time Ehline made its mark locally as builders of trophy homes in Cielo and Cielo Vista in Rancho Mirage, Norman Estates at PGA WEST, The Estates at Point Happy Ranch, The Village, The Hideaway and The Quarry in La Quinta. It

developed distinctive projects in Mirada Estates, Dominion and Cielo Azul in Rancho Mirage and built many of the ingenious ALTA homes in Palm Springs. Ehline has future plans for many commercial projects in the valley.

The Ehline brothers' commitment to the Coachella Valley is also evidenced in their work with Olive Crest Homes and Services for Abused Children, an organization that will ultimately include four homes, a private school and a recreational area.

Along the way there have been many awards such as a Gold Nugget for Norman Estates from the Pacific Coast Builders Conference. However, the biggest accomplishment has been in creating a dynamic environment for their staff, associates and clients.

Fitness Forever Personal Training & Nutrition

Ingo Logé's dedication to being fit forever began in Detroit, Mich., when as a youngster, he and his grandmother would tune in Jack La Lanne's TV show for their daily workout. He would also spend long days gardening.

"This taught me the essential value of both strength and endurance. Those early lessons assisted me in the enjoyment of successful athletic endeavors," Logé says.

As the owner of Fitness Forever in Palm Desert, Logé applies his unique perspective and approach to personal fitness training in a non-threatening environment. His artfully decorated facility boasts three private training rooms.

"The entire room of state-of-the-art equipment is basically for you to maximize your exercise time in privacy."

There is even a Power Plate, one of today's most unique fitness and rehabilitation devices that relies on advanced vibration technology for a 10-minute workout.

A Certified Personal Fitness Trainer with the National Academy of Sports Medicine, he is also certified as a C.H.E.K Institute Holistic Lifestyle Coach. During his more than 26 years of athletic and fitness experience, he has been the recipient of two Presidential Fitness Awards. He has been involved in training programs for the physically challenged as well as a U.S. Special Forces Team.

Education has always been at the forefront for Logé. He is a consultant and lecturer to national fitness franchises as well as to Fortune 500 companies. Locally he has conducted life-changing programs for associates at the JW Marriott Desert Springs and Renaissance Esmeralda.

One of the popular activities he has initiated is grocery tours so that clients have a better understanding of the foods they choose. Logé also offers phone consultations and on-line training for those looking for coaching and support. In addition, he is available to design custom gyms for both homes and corporations.

An experienced tri athlete, his fitness heroes are his clients. Personal training and proper nutrition are core components in programs such as his eight-week How to Eat, Move & Be Healthy.

Steve Pufpaf, market director of group sales for Western Region Marriott International, has high praise for Logé. "I know that without a doubt I have changed my life and how I approach nutrition and my overall health. Certain people make a big impact on who we become in life and I thank you...."

"There is no magic pill," Logé says. "I am here to provide instruction and leadership but you must take responsibility for your life and body."

KDI Stoneworks

Paul and Annie Klein, founders and owners of KDI Stoneworks, the largest stone and tile company in the Coachella Valley, profess that both their personal and professional success delightfully parallels that of their beloved La Quinta.

It is a parallel that meshes both the charm of the historic and the excitement of the community's extraordinary growth.

The couple met when Annie was working in the accounting department for a local builder. Paul, an independent tile contractor, would stop by and visit with Annie when he was there for business. Romance blossomed and in December 1990 they were married at the legendary La Quinta Hotel.

Soon Paul was busy with installation projects at Lake La Quinta. Annie, who had quit her accounting job when they married, would haul tile in the family pick up. A few employees came on board and there was a need for someone to assist customers with design. Annie Klein Design was launched and although they drew clients from throughout the Coachella Valley, Lake La Quinta became their base of operations.

Their company's steady progression continued as Paul began doing large custom jobs that involved floors, showers and countertops. Annie Klein Design became Klein Design Inc. and when they began fabricating countertops in 1999, the name was changed to KDI Stoneworks.

Today KDI Stoneworks has 500 employees, an exquisite design studio in Bermuda Dunes and two buildings in Palm Desert for a total of 62,000 square feet.

"We still think of ourselves as a mom and pop operation," Paul says. "Annie handles the financial end of the business and I concentrate on operations and sales. We owe a great deal of our success to the phenomenal growth of the area."

Although the company continues to work with major national home builders, it maintains its strong niche with custom work which it considers its foundation. Custom homes in luxury country club communities such as The Estancias at Rancho La Quinta, Andalusia at Coral Mountain, and The Summit at PGA West have all benefited from KDI Stoneworks' dedication to quality craftsmanship.

KDI installs ceramic tile and stone flooring and has added a carpeting division. Shower stalls and kitchen and bathroom countertops of tile or stone slabs are still a major part of their work. Exterior cladding is also popular with customers seeking rustic facades. Sources are worldwide as materials are imported from Brazil, Turkey, Italy and Israel. Fabrication is done at the Bermuda Dunes facility.

Almost all of new business is based on referrals. The Kleins consider customer service a vital component of everything they do. They credit their Midwestern beginnings, Annie is from Kansas and Paul grew up in Nebraska, for their strong work ethic and values.

"We grew up in homes where you follow through," Annie says. "You can count on what we say."

This credo trickles down to staff as the Kleins are adamant about keeping their word.

"If we're going to be five or 10 minutes late to a job, then we ask our employees to call ahead and inform the customer," Paul says. "This speaks volumes about the way we do business. And it says we value your time."

Many of their employees, having learned a trade through internal training programs, have been with them for years. They are recognized annually for their service and participate in the company's numerous charitable activities.

Not the least of which is KDI Kares, a charitable foundation created by the Kleins. It is not unusual during the holiday season to see employees knitting scarves and hats for the Coachella Valley Rescue Mission. And they also collect toys for the Marine Corps Air Ground Combat Center's

"We owe a great deal of our success to the phenomenal growth of the area."

Enduring Families program in Twentynine Palms. Vendors and customers are invited to participate.

"We have been so blessed," Annie says. "It is our obligation to give back to the community."

Paul has recently been named president of Building Horizons, a valley-wide non profit that sponsors high school students and teaches them a trade as they build several houses each year that are subsequently sold to low-income families.

When not working or giving back, the Kleins enjoy the fitness facilities at Rancho La Quinta and four-mile morning walks. They have made their home in La Quinta for years.

"We like to travel with our family, but no matter where we go, it can't compare with La Quinta," Paul enthuses. "Living in La Quinta is like being on vacation all the time."

Their blended family includes four children, two reside in La Quinta. Daughter Lauri is a senior vice president at KDI and son Dustin, along with his wife Dana, owns Old Town Cellar in Old Town La Quinta.

PHOTOGRAPHER TAYLOR SHERRILL

"This is home," says Annie. "We can watch our employees' kids play soccer at the park, get together with our friends, family, grandkids...it's all here in La Quinta."

La Quinta Resort & Club

Imagine adorable Shirley Temple hunting Easter eggs on the hotel lawn. Picture the glamorous Ginger Rogers, radiant as she selects this quiet sanctuary for her nuptials to French actor Jacques Bergerac. There's Frank Capra penning many of his film classics at the hotel, a place that he believed to be both lucky and inspirational.

"It was the kind of place everyone was looking for…a wonderful green oasis in the middle of the desert, and it was absolutely private," Capra said.

Since its opening in 1926, little and much have changed. Today, La Quinta Resort & Club, now part of The Waldorf Astoria Collection™, is still an enchanting respite for the famous. It is still a retreat with a Hollywood history that continues as today's celebrities and industry moguls return for much the same reasons as their predecessors.

Although the resort has carefully expanded to 800 guest rooms and suites, it retains the charm of earlier times. Each room is designed as a Spanish-style casita and includes a luxurious Cama de Sueños (Bed of Dreams), which is delicately citrus-scented nightly by turndown attendants. The fragrances of grapefruit, orange and lemon trees and 700,000 palettes of flowers planted annually fill the air.

The resort offers a variety of activities. Guests can choose from five award-winning 18-hole golf courses, including the newly renovated Mountain™, Dunes™ and PGA WEST's Norman, Nicklaus Tournament and Stadium. There is also a state-of-the-art fitness center and the 23,000-square-foot Spa La Quinta with indoor/outdoor massage and treatment rooms, an outdoor lounging courtyard with fireplace and wading fountain and outdoor baths. A premier tennis club boasts 13 courts, private lessons, clinics and a tennis pro shop. The courts include five hydro-courts and all are lighted for night play. There are 41 pools, 53 hot spas and an extraordinary family-oriented signature pool soon to debut. For little ones, there is Camp La Quinta, a kid's camp with daily activities.

In addition, there are three remarkable restaurants, Azur, Twenty 6 and Adobe Grill, and 11 exquisite shops throughout the resort.

From intimate board meetings to groups of 1,800, the resort offers more than 66,000 square feet of function space, including two ballrooms and four outdoor venues.

Whether you are planning your next vacation, business trip or need to book your next event, come to La Quinta Resort & Club and discover the beauty, mystique and what Hollywood's finest have known for almost a century — We treat you famously.

La Quinta Chamber of Commerce

The Mission Statement of the La Quinta Chamber of Commerce is to promote and enhance business growth, civic well-being and a sound quality of life.

For more than five decades the La Quinta Chamber of Commerce has served the business community of the Coachella Valley. The Chamber was originally incorporated on March 24, 1950. The secretary at the time was Frances Hack and her father was issued the first chamber membership card. Since that time, the chamber has grown at a phenomenal rate and now retains over 760 members.

We are very proud of our long tradition of serving the needs of local businesses. Membership Services, Legislative, Events & Programs, and Education Committees provide specific services for our members. The committees welcome all who wish to serve on them.

The strategic objectives of the Chamber are to create a strong local economy, promote the community, provide networking opportunities, represent the interests of business in government, take political action when necessary to protect our members.

The chamber has tremendous opportunities for advertising such as our GEM

Newsletter with a circulation of 20,000. The newsletter is mailed to all La Quinta residents, businesses and chamber members. The newsletter has been expanded to 24 pages, all color. Each issue features two full pages of photographs of our members at recent Chamber events. Other advertising opportunities are internet, business directory, map, and mid-month mailers.

Our programs consist of the bi-monthly Mayor's Luncheons, Power Lunches, and Breakfast Networks. Each of these provide network and sponsorship opportunities.

With an average attendance over 100 people, our monthly Mixers showcase member businesses. Each year the Chamber hosts the Annual Mayor's Cup Golf Tournament. One hundred forty four players register for the tournament and dinner. A six hole putting contest kicks off the day. Wonderful prizes are donated by our generous members.

April brings the annual BizNet Symposium & Showcase. This event gives each business a chance to promote their products and services to over 1,000 attendees in a convention-style setting. This Showcase has become the largest business expo in the valley.

The Chamber of Commerce also participates in City events; picnics, concerts and other community gatherings. The La Quinta Visitors Center is located in the Chamber office and is managed by our very competent staff.

It is our ambition to convey a message to each and every person who visits the Chamber office that, La Quinta truly is the "Gem of the Desert." Visit us at: www.lqchamber.com.

Law Offices of Julia E. Burt A.P.C.

While Julia E. Burt was an undergraduate student at the University of Wisconsin in Madison majoring in accounting, she found that it was a class in business law that really caught her interest. Today, Burt enjoys the rare combination of having both a CPA and a law degree, having earned the latter from Western State University College of Law in Fullerton.

This has proved ideal for her law practice which specializes in estate planning involving trusts, wills, probate and conservatorships, as well as in corporate/business law and select tax matters.

"At the end of the day everything comes down to a legal matter be it death, marriage or business," Burt says.

Burt's boutique firm emphasizes a caring, personal approach. Each client works directly with her.

"We are a full-service firm. Part of what we do is to educate our clients so they understand the "what" and "why" of our advice. To do that, we must take time to understand your short-term and long-term goals, and your family, to ensure we deliver sound legal solutions based on your unique circumstances. Our motto is: Practicing law; perfecting results."

Burt is adamant in promoting estate planning. She educates against the do-nothing approach; it costs the beneficiaries of an estate more in probate fees, which are based on a percent of the gross estate, and precious time.

When it comes to corporate formation and counsel, Burt's firm assists in establishing business entities such as a Limited Liability Company (LLC) or a Corporation (C, S and PSC).

A relatively new resident of La Quinta, Burt has quickly become an enthusiastic ambassador for her community. Her law offices reflect this with a series of historic photographs gracing the walls.

"I visited the La Quinta Historical Society to find these pictures. I think that wherever you are you should honor the area. I love the mountains of La Quinta and my office enjoys one of the best views of Point Happy."

Burt and her golden retriever, Aspen, are frequent hikers of the Santa Rosa Mountains. Having vacationed in the Coachella Valley for many years, it was the tranquil desert environment and its abundant golf that convinced Burt and her husband, Randall, to relocate here from Lake Tahoe.

For Burt, practicing law and living in La Quinta is just another great combination.

Legacy Villas℠ at La Quinta

Neighboring the historic La Quinta Resort & Club®, Legacy Villas is an extension of the Old World charm for which the resort is legendary. Tucked into its own canyon on 47 breathtaking desert acres, this 24-hour guard-gated enclave echoes the resort's Spanish-style architecture with hand-troweled white stucco, barrel-tile roofs and the signature bright blue shutters and window trim.

In all, there are only 280 Townhomes and Villas. The Villas are turnkey furnished and available with 2 to 3 bedrooms. Townhomes are 3-bedroom with 2.75 to 3.5 baths. All boast glorious views of the Santa Rosa Mountains, lushly landscaped paseos, pools or fountains.

Standard features include solid granite countertops, KitchenAid® appliances, Kohler® fixtures, gas log fireplaces and energy-efficient windows with low-E glass and classic wood plantation shutters.

The grand Spanish-style architecture is again evident in the elegant 11,000-square-foot clubhouse which has an inviting bar and grill, fully appointed lounge and meeting rooms, and a state-of-the-art fitness center. This is a neighborhood that celebrates the outdoors with enchanting paseos dotted with a date palm hammock garden, fragrant fruit trees, and many cascading fountains. There are 12 swimming pools and 11 spas, including three huge resort pools at the clubhouse facility.

But there is even more to take advantage of in this amenity-rich community. Homeowners are granted the opportunity to activate a social membership to The Citrus Club at La Quinta Resort & Club™. If they choose to do so, they are entitled to full use of the resort's world-famous tennis and fitness facilities and receive discounts at the resort's luxury spa, restaurants, golf courses and gift

shop. They can even order maid and room service as club members.

Another very unique feature of Legacy Villas is that because the development is zoned as resort commercial, leasing options are available to homeowners.

Legacy Villas provides its owners and their guests the convenience and flexibility that only a private, luxury, lifestyle resort can. Legacy Villas, resort living at its best.

Legacy Rooms Express

When La Quinta's first furniture store, the 35,000-square-foot Legacy Rooms Express, opened its doors in September 2006, it was cause for celebration.

It wasn't long before the full-service store attracted a widespread demographic that welcomed the quality, selection, value and customer service unique to Legacy Rooms Express.

"We are all about offering great products at a great price. We try to be a total solution for our customers," says Eric Foucrier, who is a co-partner with Philip Linder of Linder's Furniture, Legacy Furniture and Legacy Rooms Express. Headquartered in Garden Grove, Calif., the 25-year-old company operates 10 showrooms, including three in the Coachella Valley.

"We want to 'wow' customers with a special visual experience. We have created an inviting environment that is creative, comfortable and friendly," Foucrier says. In addition to furniture, the store carries a wide selection of mattresses, accessories and home theater electronics.

Needs can vary from full-time residents looking for furnishings to second home owners in the market for a houseful of durable furniture for a rental. Customers can also opt for custom-made furniture. There is even an area dedicated to rooms for kids and teens. Plus, the store features a Legacy Showcase to provide customers with a sampling of designer furniture for less. The Home Theater Center provides residents with a one-stop source for home theater needs.

Everyone can take advantage of same day delivery service because the company has its own 100,000-square-foot warehouse in Cathedral City with just under $7 million of furniture in stock and ready for immediate delivery.

Another unique feature is the store's strong price guarantee. If you find any item at a lower price, Legacy Rooms Express will beat it by 10%. Plus there are always attractive financing programs in place for those interested. Should you wish decorating

assistance, seasoned interior designers are available for complimentary house calls.

Foucrier attributes much of the store's success to its enthusiastic staff of professionals who receive on going training to keep abreast of the latest styles and technology.

"You can feel the difference when you walk into the store."

Already Legacy Rooms Express has made a difference having donated furniture for two Habitat for Humanity homes. In addition, not only is the store the Coachella Valley's largest drop-off location for the Toys for Tots holiday program, it will give anyone who brings in a new, unwrapped toy their choice of either a $100 gift certificate toward an in-store purchase or a Free Hitachi DVD player.

Old Town Cellar

Since March 2004, Old Town Cellar has been delighting customers in picturesque Old Town La Quinta. Dustin Nichols, who along with his wife, Dana, owns the establishment, felt that the growing community was ripe for this unique store.

"There was nothing like it in the area," Dustin says. "We have something for everyone with a great selection of wines, competitively priced from $6 to $600."

Today Old Town Cellar is considered the hip, chic place to go. Customers can sip wines by the glass at the popular Wine Bar or they can opt for a tasting-sized portion. Two gourmet platters are also available; one features homemade, hand-dipped chocolate truffles from the Palm Springs Candy Company while the other is a selection of cheeses, crackers and dried meats from The Market on El Paseo. There is also a small humidor housing some of the world's finest cigars.

Although the store specializes in California boutique wines handcrafted from small, family-owned wineries, there are also wines from Oregon, Washington, Italy, France, Australia, New Zealand, Argentina, South Africa and Chile.

The ambiance is sophisticated, comfortable and inviting. There is a lounge area with overstuffed leather chairs. The sleek, 25-foot granite bar provides plenty of room for gathering with friends. Walls are graced with a rotating selection of fine art on loan from The French Collection, a nearby gallery.

Open daily, Old Town Cellar is available for private and semi-private parties in the store or in your home.

For Dustin, his store is a culmination of 15 years of experience in the food and beverage industry. After graduating from Kansas State University in Manhattan, Kan., with a major in business, he moved to the Coachella Valley where his parents have lived for 20 years. Along the way he also went to bartending school. Stints with the Hotel Indian Wells and at the Ritz-Carlton Huntington Hotel in Pasadena were followed by management positions at Twin Palms Restaurant in Newport Beach and at Aqua, an upscale restaurant located in the Bellagio at Las Vegas.

At Old Town Cellar, service is always at the forefront. There is even a golf cart to shuttle customers to their cars or hotel and for deliveries to nearby country clubs.

"I found that the service industry and dealing with people fit me well," Dustin says. "My customers like dealing with the owner. It is not about the dollars. It is all about relationships."

PGA WEST®

When PGA WEST, the extraordinary master-planned community, premiered in 1984, it was considered one of a kind. Today, its more than 1,600 members will attest that it is still unmatched, especially when it comes to its diversity of golf courses.

One might say that PGA WEST and the City of La Quinta grew together, for over the years, worldwide media exposure enjoyed by this prestigious golf community also promoted the inviting La Quinta lifestyle.

PGA WEST "The Western Home of Golf in America®," offers six world championship courses: Three private courses—Arnold Palmer Private, Jack Nicklaus Private and Tom Weiskopf Private—and three courses that are open to Member and Resort play—Stadium Course, Jack Nicklaus Tournament and Greg Norman. All of the PGA WEST golf courses were designed by five of the world's finest golf course architects.

Ask Jennifer Jenkins, director of marketing and membership sales, what constitutes a great club and she will say "the members."

"This is a very comfortable, down-to-earth group of people. It is one of my favorite things about PGA WEST," Jenkins says.

Indeed, it is all about the members who enjoy three clubhouses. There is also a Health and Racquet Club with tennis courts of grass, clay and hard surfaces, a croquet lawn and a state-of-the-art fitness center. Trail hikes, 5K runs and exercise programs geared to members are also part of the fun. There's even a Kid's Klub that keeps youngsters busy five days a week during the season.

For adults, there are more than 300 social activities each year encompassing everything from watercolor classes to bridge games and holiday parties.

PHOTOGRAPHER EVAN SCHILLER

One of the long-standing, member-supported programs is Toys for Tots, a holiday campaign sponsored by the Marine Corps Air Ground Combat Center in Twenty-nine Palms. Members donate toys that are distributed to needy children throughout the desert. In addition, 20 Marines join members at the club for a holiday dinner.

Memberships are as varied as the activities. One can select a Premier Social Membership that provides access to the Health and Racquet Club, dining and all social events. A Premier Sport Membership offers limited golf access to all PGA WEST golf courses. Premier Sport Members pay the member/guest greens fees per round and will enjoy all social membership amenities. A Premier Golf Membership allows for unlimited play on all six courses along with social membership amenities. A Premier Desert Membership adds the Social and Golf Membership privileges at the La Quinta Resort & Club to the Premier Golf Membership at PGA WEST. For those under age 40, PGA WEST offers Junior Memberships. PGA WEST is definitely one of a kind.

Radio Active

At first glance, the audio-visual products in Radio Active's showroom may seem like something out of the Jetsons, but look again and it's very much today. Mark Reulman, owner and president of Radio Active, is all about ushering his clients into the convenience that comes from incorporating the latest technology into their lifestyles. Reulman, who has been in business in the Coachella Valley for more than two decades, started out as an auto mechanic. He knows how things work.

"The whole idea is to make the customer's life simple," Reulman says. "People are apprehensive about new technology so it's up to us to create a user-friendly environment for them."

Customers can get a sampling of the marvelous possibilities that await by visiting the Radio Active facility which is shared with Desert Life Styles, Designs by Kaveh. Reulman and Kaveh Daryaie have created a 2,700-square-foot smart home that is a state-of-the-art showcase of their sophisticated talents. While Kaveh concentrated on the interior design, Reulman focused on the wiring. The showroom is truly a home with a fully equipped kitchen, bar, living and dining room, powder room, bedroom and home theater.

However, the switch is that there are no switches. Walk into the bedroom and note that the electronic components consist of in-wall and in-ceiling speakers. Everything is fully automated with a universal remote control that ties in appliances, lighting, security, Jacuzzi, music, TV, and other devices, that can control the home environment while there or away.

Radio Active is also known for its custom home theater systems. Once again everything is user-friendly designed so that one button can dim the lights, open the curtain, drop the screen and activate the projector. In addition, there is a large selection of modular, reclining, home theater seating that can be customized by style, fabric and configuration. Some come with massage features perfect for relaxing under a fiber-optic starlight ceiling.

In addition, the family owned and operated company also installs

intercom, security and surveillance systems.

"We pride ourselves on our customer service and the quality of our installations. Many of our employees have been with us a long time."

Reulman hopes that buyers and builders of new homes will become more educated and insist that homes are wired for the future. He sites Andalusia at Coral Mountain as being an excellent example of in-wall wiring that Radio Active installed.

"The quality infrastructure is built into those homes. As upgrades come along, those folks are going to be very happy."

Solis Wealth Management Inc.

 Greg Solis, president and founder of Solis Wealth Management, Inc. in La Quinta is not your traditional stockbroker. His full-service firm introduces itself to prospective clients by asking what they value most in life. For Solis, it is about sitting down with clients and building a foundation based on their needs, goals, risk tolerance, and what the best odds of success are to accomplish what they value most.

"I want to help my clients make smart decisions with their money, which means not only helping them achieve financial success, but more importantly achieve personal significance in their life. To accomplish this, I must provide the best advice and service available in the financial industry…and I must do it with the highest level of competence and integrity."

His firm's six-step process includes a complimentary consultation to determine if Solis feels he can add value to the client's situation while establishing a mutually beneficial relationship. Next, a comprehensive plan, compiled from information provided, addresses current assets and a recommended asset allocation model. At this stage, such things as estate, retirement, and life insurance planning, as well as tax strategizing, college funding, debt financing, long-term care insurance, and cash flow analysis are reviewed. If Solis and the client feel they can establish a mutually beneficial relationship, then the transfer process and document signing are completed followed by an implementation plan. Although not mandatory, Solis encourages quarterly reviews to ensure that the plan is on track.

After graduating from the University of California, Los Angeles, with a double major in political science and history, Solis worked for Paychex, Inc., Merrill Lynch, and Wachovia Securities. During his nine years with Linsco/Private Ledger (LPL), he was named to the firm's prestigious Chairman's Club, an honor awarded to the top 5% of the firm's approximately 6,500 advisors, based on revenue. Solis is a Registered Representative with and offering securities through Linsco/Private Ledger (LPL) Member NASD/SIPC.

Born and raised in Palm Desert, Solis has a strong commitment to the Coachella Valley. Locally, Solis Wealth Management provides an infrastructure for charitable organizations that include Highways and Hedges, Cornerstone Community Church, FCA, and Justice for Children International. Organizations are invited to use the firm's office space, machines and desks.

"I have personally been blessed beyond anything I can imagine," Solis says. "We want to give back. My staff and I love making a positive impact on the world around us."

When not helping others, Solis enjoys spending time with his wife, Monica, and their three young children, Jack, Nicole, and Emily.

South West Concepts

As a young boy growing up in Palm Desert, Steve Nieto was fascinated watching College of the Desert being built. He would stop playing with his friends to pick up metal slugs, which he pretended were money. He liked the feel of copper wire scraps and the smell of fresh wood shavings. The detritus of construction left a major imprint on the youngster who knew early on what he wanted to do.

After graduating from California State Polytechnic University, Pomona, with a bachelor's degree in architecture, Nieto returned to the Coachella Valley to pursue his dream. Along the way he became licensed in the state of California as a general contractor.

Step by step Nieto expanded his business. Today, with more than 20 years of experience in design, construction management and development, he is the owner and principal designer of South West Concepts, an architectural design firm renowned for its luxury residential design, commercial office and retail centers.

"I love La Quinta and knew the town would do well," Nieto says. "The community's growth paralleled my business so it just seemed right to locate our offices in the village of La Quinta."

South West Concepts' impact on the community can be delightfully experienced today in the second phase of Old Town and Coronel Plaza. The two-story commercial buildings house retail on the first floors with office space above. Other projects include Plaza Estado which is currently under construction and Sun Vista Plaza which is slated to start construction the beginning of next year.

The Santa Barbara-style architecture is a distinctive aesthetic of ornamental wrought iron balconies and stairway rails, recessed niches with iron bars and colorful decorative tiles. Garden courtyards with soothing fountains enhance the walkways that wend past shops, restaurants and galleries.

"We are meticulous about the details," Nieto says. "There are definitive elements about the second phase of Old Town that created more of a village environment with different building shapes and profiles that are at the same time homogeneous yet unique."

Residential design is also a major part of South West Concepts' extensive portfolio with several custom home projects in the prestigious communities of The Hideaway, Bighorn and Mirada, among others. Popular design trends include Tuscan, Spanish Revival and Desert Contemporary.

"We are a full-service firm," Nieto says. "Together with our team of professionals and consultants we can provide a total package to include site design, landscaping, structural and civil engineering. It is always our goal to provide quality design and working drawings that will create 'Projects of Distinction' and maximize the investments of our clients."

Southern Hills Real Estate & Development

Back in the mid '80s, Jeff and John Read earned a solid reputation for quality, building more than 1300 homes in the San Francisco Bay Area. No strangers to the Coachella Valley, the Read brothers were frequent visitors to the Palm Desert home of their parents, Fran and Bob, who later moved to PGA WEST to be among the first members.

By the late 80's both Jeff and John had homes at PGA WEST and then created their new company, Southern Hills Development. A focus on building relationships as well as stunning homes led to The Summit at PGA WEST, their showcase. This extraordinary 60-home enclave situated around four holes of the Tom Weiskopf Private Course demonstrates their attention to detail and quality craftsmanship.

Recently a real estate division was created to specialize in new, resale and lease homes in luxury country club communities. Southern Hills Real Estate & Development boasts an extensive portfolio with custom homes in the Hideaway, Peninsula Park, Tradition Golf Club, The Enclave, and PGA WEST. Southern Hills Real Estate & Development's hallmarks are quality, creativity and accessibility.

"We live and are headquartered in La Quinta so we are readily available to both current and prospective homeowners," Jeff says.

Today there are four generations of Reads who call La Quinta home. Parents Fran and Bob live at The Summit. Jeff and his wife, Cheryl, a Southern Hills realtor, live there as well. Their daughter Anna is the receptionist for Southern Hills Real Estate and Development.

John and his wife, Ellen, recently moved into their new home in the Summit. Ellen is the director of marketing and design. Their son, Mike, is in charge of operations and also lives there with his wife, Brittany, and their daughter, Catie. Son Greg Read is a licensed realtor with Southern Hills and also calls La Quinta home.

The Read brothers love their work. The homes they build are an expression of their talent and character.

"We are a small family business. We can take the time to listen carefully to the wants and desires of our customers, then together build their dream," John says.

Southern Hills Real Estate & Development is truly a family affair with an endearing dedication to La Quinta. The Read family will be building dreams in La Quinta for many years to come.

Vacation Pools Inc.

Gerald Hampton, president and owner of Vacation Pools Inc., got an early start in the family-owned business. When he was just eight years old, he began helping his dad at the company's headquarters, which at that time was located in the Inland Empire.

The Hamptons had a second home in the Coachella Valley and had been vacationing there for years, so it was but a natural progression to relocate the operation to Indio in 2005.

Now 30 years in business and going strong, Vacation Pools Inc. has complemented the area's phenomenal growth by building quality custom pools for custom homes, design centers, residential, commercial, builders of communities, apartment complexes, homeowners associations and fitness centers.

"We deliver high quality but with a personal touch," Hampton says. "Our customer service blows everyone away. We believe our expertise in construction, experience in all types of challenges and our effort to provide unparalleled service to all customers is unmatched in the pool industry."

Products include artificial rock pools and slides, barbecues and firepits, patio covers, beach entry and tanning ledges, and fountains as well as commercial, contemporary, freeform, infinity edge, natural rock and small backyard pools. In addition, Vacation Pools Inc. has its own nursery and professional landscape design division.

"Anything you want in the backyard, we can do," Hampton says.

Clients include the prestigious resort communities of Terra Lago in Indio, Lake La Quinta Country Club and Legacy Villas in La Quinta, where they designed and installed the charming paseo fountains and community pools and spas.

There are lifetime structural warranties on pools and spas, and ample time is allocated through on-site consultations to ensure that every prospects needs from a small backyard pool to a large commercial project are more than satisfactorily understood and met. A complimentary custom design that reflects the client's wishes and budget is then provided. Convenient financing is also available.

Advances in technology have allowed for a myriad of innovative pool options that include water treatment, fiber-optic lighting, spa products, remote controls and automatic cleaning systems.

"We never submit a low introductory bid and make expensive changes later. Our estimates incorporate the highest quality materials, craftsmanship and design. Efficient

buying power, swift construction time and coordination of crews make for no headaches and no cost overruns."

Hampton sets aside time for the Boys Scouts of America and for his church youth groups. With four active kids of his own, he also coaches baseball and football in La Quinta.

Index: Those Who Make a Difference